COMMIT
&
DELIVER

ALSO BY CYRUS FREIDHEIM

The Star of Africa

Notes from Grampa

The Trillion-Dollar Enterprise

COMMIT & DELIVER

On the Frontlines of Management Consulting

CYRUS FREIDHEIM

Matt Holt Books
An Imprint of BenBella Books, Inc.
Dallas, TX

BenBella Books, Inc.
10440 N. Central Expressway
Suite 800
Dallas, TX 75231
benbellabooks.com
Send feedback to feedback@benbellabooks.com

BenBella is a federally registered trademark.
Matt Holt and logo are trademarks of BenBella Books.

Printed in the United States of America
10 9 8 7 6 5 4 3 2 1

Library of Congress Control Number: 2021020364
ISBN 9781953295675 (print)
ISBN 9781637740019 (electronic)

Copyediting by Rebecca Taff
Proofreading by James Fraleigh and Lisa Story
Indexing by WordCo Indexing Services, Inc.
Text design by Katie Hollister
Text composition by PerfecType, Nashville, TN
Cover design by James Reyman
Printed by Lake Book Manufacturing

Special discounts for bulk sales are available.
Please contact bulkorders@benbellabooks.com.

Mitzi, Lynn, Stephen, Scott

and

My Many Mentors from
Childhood Through Retirement

"Grampa, congratulations on your new book, *Commit & Deliver.*
We can't wait till we are old enough to read it!"
—Luke, Ethan , Madison, Juliette, Louis,
Edouard, Alexander, Leo, and Ana

CONTENTS

PREFACE

It was the fifth inning in game three of the 1932 World Series at Wrigley Field in Chicago, with the score tied at 4–4. The great Babe Ruth of the New York Yankees came to bat and the Cubs' dugout and fans went wild—screaming and even throwing tomatoes at him. Ruth took two strikes, paused, and pointed his bat at the center-field bleachers. On the next pitch Ruth hit the most famous home run in baseball history to the back of the center-field bleachers. He *committed*, and he *delivered*.

In August 1981, almost seven months after Ronald Reagan was inaugurated as the fortieth president of the United States, the air traffic controllers' union (PATCO) went on strike, illegally. He told them publicly that the strike was illegal and that anyone remaining on strike in forty-eight hours would be fired. He repeated his order several times during the next two days. At the expiration of forty-eight hours, he fired the 11,000 controllers who remained on strike. In the interim, plans were put together to manage the nation's airways with supervisors, non-striking controllers, and military controllers so the airline system operated safely with 80 percent capacity for the time it took to hire and train new controllers. PATCO was decertified, and the fired controllers were banned from working as controllers for life. No one ever doubted that President Reagan was a man of his word after that. He *committed* and *delivered*.

While these are dramatic examples, they do illustrate the power of Commit and Deliver. It is a simple concept—you say you are going to do something, and you do it. You don't equivocate with either. The result—people will learn to believe you, to trust you. Bullies and opponents will fear you. Everyone will respect you and understand that your word is your bond and that you are a person on whom they can depend.

While the concept is simple, execution is not so easy. The consequences of committing and *not* delivering can be serious in many ways, including damaging your reputation for reliability and trust—in addition to making a mess of things. Do not draw red lines or make big promises without knowing you are *able* to deliver and *will*. As in the case of President Reagan and PATCO, he had to be convinced of his legal right to fire the strikers and the feasibility of operating our airways safely without 11,000 PATCO controllers. Before you make a commitment, you need to do the research and planning necessary to know how you can deliver. No time for hunches, guesses, or shooting from the hip. A commitment is just that, a *commitment.*

Who likes people who commit and deliver? In business: your boss, your board, your shareholders, your bankers, your suppliers, your unions, your partners, your subordinates, your teammates, your regulators, your community, and most important, your customers and clients. In your personal life: every member of your immediate and extended family, starting with your spouse, wants you to commit and deliver, as do your organizations, your clubs, your schoolmates, your teammates in sports, all those who depend on you. When is commit and deliver important to you? Always.

Who *doesn't* like you to commit and deliver? Your competition, opponents, and critics. You will infuriate them.

This book was written for anyone interested in learning how business is conducted from the perspectives of a management consultant, a CEO, and a member of the board of directors.

Specifically, for:

Teenagers who are wondering what the business world is like and are considering college—whether to go, which colleges to apply to, what to major in, whether to go full-time.

College students who want practical context about the business world to augment their theoretical studies, who are as concerned about what kind of people they should become as what career path they should follow, who are deciding whether to change a major or school.

Young adults who are considering career options—selecting the first career job, debating whether to go to graduate school, curious about management consulting, wondering whether they should accept unconventional assignments, making plans to accelerate their career progression.

Mid-career professionals who are considering career changes, who may be stalled or bored or uncomfortable in their current situation, who are faced with a tough career-altering decision, who are wondering, "Is this all there is?"

Professionals nearing or starting retirement, who are nervous about retiring, who wish to continue an active, involved, interesting life, who would rather "wear out than rust out."

Grandfathers who are considering writing their own stories.

INTRODUCTION

L ast year, *Notes from Grampa* was printed and distributed to my family and a few friends. I wrote that book on my life and the lessons learned in response to my children, who told me: "Your young grandchildren will never get to know you, and they are interested."

While I was writing the book, it became clear that my experiences as a management consultant, CEO, and board member gave me useful perspectives that would have been really helpful during my career journey of over fifty years.

Commit & Deliver uses the framework of my career to explore how career and personal decisions can be prepared for and made; how to grow professionally; how to think through complex business problems from a practitioner's perspective. Much of my career was devoted to working with CEOs as a management consultant and as a board member to help them improve the direction and performance of their companies. I had the opportunity to live in several countries and work in multiple industries, which gave me an understanding of business in different cultures, forms of government, and economic systems.

Most college students have little idea of career opportunities in business. I had almost none. All I knew was that I did not want to be a chemical engineer, even though I spent four years getting that degree. Fortunately, I discovered the world of business and decided to get an

MBA following my four years in the Navy—an obligation in return for their financing my college education. Chapter two tracks my decision process that ultimately landed me at Booz Allen Hamilton. I hadn't even heard of management consulting while in college. This book gives a hands-on view of what consultants do, how they interact with their corporate clients, and what it takes to become a good consultant. It paints a picture of what life is like at the bottom of the business career ladder, what is expected, what you must bring to the table, and what it takes to move up the ladder in virtually any industry.

In retrospect, I recognize that a number of issues over which you will have little or no control will impact your careers and will present great opportunities and major risks. This book discusses the turbulent times through which I lived and worked. Recognizing and understanding those issues that you will confront will enable you to navigate your career more successfully. Progress in almost all human endeavors is achieved by understanding and building on the past. Almost all major inventions and research breakthroughs are built on existing knowledge.

The key to innovation is the ability to see *what can be* from today's technology, markets, and financial conditions.

The business, political, technological, and social world that I experienced changed as much as any time in history. The rate of change that you will face will undoubtedly be even greater. An understanding of what happened in the last century is essential for you to prepare yourselves for the century you will experience. This book deals with the past through my experiences and observations and identifies the major forces that, I believe, you must confront.

Turbulence, chaos, and change create opportunities.

A number of trends are already clear, though the direction and impact they will ultimately have on business are not clear. Your generation will take the controls and steer society. We know that globalization and the technology revolution are just gaining steam. A number of industries will be disrupted by new technologies and new strategies. I saw it happen in autos, telecommunications, energy, airlines, distribution, and newspapers; you will experience disruption in healthcare, education, transportation, energy, manufacturing, retail, distribution, and many more areas of your world. You will be faced with challenges to free-market capitalism and social and political upheaval driven by increasing income disparity. Your workplace will be different, driven by shifting morals, ethics, and behavioral norms. As I was making final edits to this book, the coronavirus pandemic struck the world a devastating blow. Ways of conducting business will undoubtedly change, as will our everyday activities. An understanding of these forces will put you ahead of those who do not recognize how business will be changed by them. When you get frustrated, just remember that chaos is the breeding ground for opportunities. You can shape the future.

Finally, I offer my perspectives on what's important and what's not, on how you should think about big decisions and new situations, both in your professional careers and personal life. My assumption is that every reader of this book is rational and will act on his or her values, principles, and interests. You should take my suggestions and lessons learned, digest them, and then develop your own set of guideposts. My purpose is not to change your life, but rather to guide you to improve it.

MY LIFE

First and foremost, I am a son, grandson, brother, husband, father, cousin, nephew, uncle, in-law, godfather, and grandfather. Shortly before he died, my father was telling me about his life, which started and was about to end on the South Side of Chicago. He had achieved many things in his eighty years. He concluded with, "Son, in the end, you have your family. Nothing in life matters more. Outside of family, nothing *really* matters."

Second, I am a businessman—for most of my career an outside consultant helping companies make themselves better. Late in my career, I became CEO of two turnarounds. My stories should be read in the context of what was going on in the country and the world at the time. While I'm not a historian and this isn't a history book, I'll provide some of that background. I've learned from every personal and business experience, and my aim is to pass many of those lessons on to you.

Third, I am a member of communities—schools and teams; the military; the church; the cities I have called home; the companies I worked with; the clubs I belonged to; the civic, business, and charitable organizations I served. I gathered many friends along the way and tried my best to be helpful, supportive, generous, and kind to everyone, particularly to those who weren't as fortunate. There were many companions on my journey, and their friendship has made my life fuller.

A few important decisions chart our lives. Some can be planned, others not. Every person is dealt a unique hand to play in life—being born into different times and circumstances, and possessing different talents, personalities, interests, ambitions, appearances, and beliefs. Every person has challenges, some small and some that appear insurmountable. To me, success in life is best measured not by what we achieve but by whether and how obstacles are overcome. My heroes are those who have overcome major setbacks and risen from the ashes to achieve what they believed was important. Happiness does not come from the absence of challenges. Unhappy people are those who do not figure out how to overcome their own particular challenges, who consider themselves victims, or who give up. In my view, we all have the obligation to be as good as we can be.

Nelson Mandela was in prison in solitary confinement unjustly for twenty-seven years in his homeland of South Africa. Every morning he would say out loud, "I am the Master of my fate. I am the Captain of my soul." He survived and became one of the greatest and most beloved leaders in history, ending apartheid in South Africa peacefully. Most would say that he was dealt an unfair, even impossible hand. Everyone should agree that he lived his life admirably and is a model for all of us as we measure the challenges we face.

Early in life we begin to judge people by characteristics we admire or value. Even at age five we are deciding what is important and what kind of person we want to be. As we get older, we refine and deepen our aspirations. Character and how others perceive us become important assets or liabilities. And it is work that we never finish. The kind of person we *want* to be will likely be the kind of person we *will* become. The challenge is to work at it constantly.

PROFESSIONS IN LIFE

Every profession in life is a trade. By profession, I mean anything you might want to become in life, whether in a career or in your personal and family life. Being a mother or a father is a profession, as are farm work, healthcare, teaching, programming, professional athletics, law, the priesthood, art, writing, carpentry, the military, and business of all sorts. We all start as beginners or apprentices at the bottom of the ladder. We go to school to build a foundation of values and basic skills that apply everywhere—like reading, writing, and math—and augment those with more career-specific education. We learn our craft over many years, working under the guidance of mentors and masters to build skills necessary in that profession. How expert we become depends mostly on how smart we are and hard we work. Having the best mentors and masters helps a lot. Focus is important. Few people become true masters of multiple crafts, as Leonardo da Vinci did.

This book describes my journey to become a master craftsman in business—where and how I developed the skills of my profession. The principles I learned apply to almost any profession you might choose. Along the way I have tried to describe what a career in business looks like—something most know too little about, even when graduating from college. Today, college students know a lot about doctors or lawyers or teachers or architects or being a parent or many other professions, but know little about a career in business. Specific lessons about business are highlighted throughout the book.

We are the sum of our choices. Sometimes we get do-overs, but usually not. Sometimes we work our hearts out and things don't go our way. And sometimes we just get lucky. This book describes my choices. The final chapter summarizes the most important lessons from my experiences.

MY TIMES

My eight decades saw a mix of economic bust and boom, devastating wars, a technology explosion that changed the way people live, social changes that tested and stretched firmly held values and behavior, political and economic revolutions, the spread of communism, devastating hunger and miraculous new medicines, the globalization of everything, spiritual upheavals, standards of living never before achieved on a massive scale, the rise and fall of nations, the advent of instantaneous communication to anyone, anywhere. This was the field on which I would play out my life.

This period has been much like other periods of human history as opposing philosophies and ambitious dictators strived to dominate. The technological innovations in communications, medicine, materials, and electronics have changed the way people live and interact. The pace of those changes and their impact on daily life are accelerating as the digital revolution permeates everything. It also appears that opposing philosophies and ambitious dictators will continue to ravage the world. Through it all, the United States of America has stood as a beacon of hope for peace and prosperity for all nations. Its strength and resources and spirit of liberty define America and its place in the world. Never lose faith in America, whether you live here or elsewhere. Put your values and energy into assuring that America retains its values and remains a force for good.

I was a witness to it all and directly involved in the evolution of several industries, the impact of globalization, and the technology blizzard. In particular, my involvement gave me interesting insights into the dramatic developments of automobiles, telecommunications, oil, airlines, and newspapers, which are discussed in the book.

MY STORY

My purpose in telling these stories is to provide guidance to those who wish to go to college and follow professional business careers. I have benefitted enormously from the counsel of people who preceded me—parents, teachers, bosses, mentors, and friends. I wish to pour everything I have learned into the minds of those who will listen so that they will have the wisdom of that experience to guide them.

My experience and observations have made me believe that the capitalist system—despite its considerable problems—provides a better standard of living and way of life than any other economic system devised and tested over human history. Similarly, I believe that democracy holds more hope for a free and fulfilling life than any other political system. Both are under fire. I encourage you to become a student of economic and political history as you form your own philosophy of life. I hope you will also conclude that capitalism and democracy based on freedom and individual responsibility are the best hope for a brighter future. I encourage you to work to assure that capitalism and democracy deliver on their promise of a better life and equal opportunity and justice for all.

The book begins in mid-career when I was the partner in charge of Booz Allen's work with the board of Chrysler Corp. in 1979 just prior to the historic government bailout of the failing automaker.

Chapter one gives an understanding of the role management consultants can play in a major crisis. It is also a shameless attempt to get you excited about business at the top level. My role in the rescue of this iconic American manufacturer taught me lessons that stuck with me throughout the rest of my life. It's an important story, not all of which has ever been told. It's got drama, politicians, unions, the media, investment bankers, and consultants, and it's a fitting tale with which to begin this book.

Enjoy the ride with me over the past eighty years—and be prepared to lead the changes in the next eighty.

Chapter One

CHRYSLER ON THE BRINK

At precisely 8:45 A.M. on a sunny Saturday in September 1979, five black SUVs pulled up to the entrances to three hotels in Washington, D.C. Each vehicle had a small crest of the Department of the Treasury of the United States on its front doors. Serious-looking men and women from Chrysler Corporation, Booz Allen Hamilton, and Salomon Brothers climbed in. As they approached the Department of the Treasury, they saw a crowd of over a hundred journalists and camera crews attempting to enter the front entrance to the building. The SUVs wound around to a rear service entry. The Deputy Secretary of the Treasury met each vehicle and directed the people to the main conference room.

The oil shock and recession that followed the fall of the Shah and establishment of the Islamic Republic of Iran in 1979 claimed many victims. Chrysler was on the verge of becoming one of the largest casualties.

A few weeks earlier, my boss, Booz Allen Hamilton's chairman, Jim Farley, received a call from the U.S. Secretary of the Treasury, G. William Miller. Miller told Farley that the government had been asked by Chrysler for a large cash infusion to prevent bankruptcy. President Jimmy Carter was motivated to help, but not if Chrysler couldn't survive. Carter was facing reelection in 1980, and his advisors warned that a Chrysler bankruptcy could result in tens of thousands of unemployed auto workers and suppliers.

Miller and Farley had known each other from Miller's years as CEO of Textron. Miller had been confirmed as Secretary of the Treasury by the Senate a few weeks earlier after serving two years as chairman of the Federal Reserve Board. Miller told him that time was critical—the government wanted an answer within two weeks to one question: Was Chrysler's strategic plan viable? Specifically, if Chrysler received the funding the company requested, would it survive? Farley told Miller he would get right back to him.

Jim Farley immediately called me to his office. I probably had the most auto experience of our senior partners.

The question wasn't whether we would do it, but rather, how. We called Richardson Dilworth, the Chrysler director to whom Miller had referred us, to get his understanding of the situation. Dilworth was the head of the Rockefeller family office, which tended to the many Rockefeller investments. He was the family's designee on the Chrysler board and was also Chrysler's lead outside director.

Dilworth's perspective was dire. Chrysler was sinking fast. Losses were mounting, and cash was running out. Dilworth pledged total cooperation and suggested we begin work immediately, the next morning. His instructions from the Secretary of the Treasury were clear—get Booz Allen.

Chrysler was the weakest link in the U.S. auto industry and had neared bankruptcy in every recession since World War II. The 1979 recession hit Chrysler with a particularly weak lineup of cars against Ford, General Motors, and the surging Japanese carmakers. Chrysler was now hemorrhaging cash.

I had just moved back to the U.S. from Europe. Farley and I discussed whom we could assemble quickly to contribute effectively to such a complex problem in such a short time. We were aware that this would be a highly visible project with considerable risks. We had to get it right, both for the client's sake and for the firm's reputation. We selected the best professionals without considering their availability. Farley used his considerable charm and got all to accept the challenge, starting immediately. Farley called Miller and told him we were on the case, but cautioned him that the amount of time was ridiculously short.

Most of the team assembled in Chrysler's Auburn Hills, Michigan, headquarters the following morning. We spent a couple of hours going over a work plan I had roughed out, assigning tasks, and sharing the information each had gathered since our call yesterday. Everyone was familiar with Chrysler's situation because it had been the number one business story in the media all year. We spent the rest of the first three days talking to every top executive (except the CEO, John Riccardo, and the president, Lee Iacocca), collecting reports, financials, and everything we thought might be relevant. We met each evening in our hotel to discuss what we had learned and what further information and questions we needed to address.

Salomon Brothers had also been retained to determine whether Chrysler's balance sheet and capital structure would be able to survive the declining cash and operating results. John Gutfreund, the CEO of Salomon, and Jim Wolfensohn, a senior partner, led the Salomon effort. We worked closely with them.

It became clear that there was no recovery plan. Like all automotive companies, they had a product plan, an annual budget, a facilities plan, a capital budget, a personnel plan, a marketing and sales plan, and many more. But there was nothing that melded all these important pieces into a single plan that laid out the steps necessary to pull Chrysler out of its nosedive and avoid bankruptcy. Nor was there a credible analysis that demonstrated how much cash was needed over what period of time. Farley and I called Dilworth with that unfortunate news—we could not judge the viability of the plan because there was no plan. Dilworth's incredible response was: "Well, can you develop a plan?" We responded: "In two weeks??" Three days had already passed. Dilworth called Treasury and explained the dilemma and was given another week. We grimaced and got to work.

Wolfensohn was in Detroit virtually every day, so we shared findings and ideas continuously. The outlook for Chrysler was bleak. Suppliers were demanding payment of past-due bills and cash on delivery for new purchases, creating a rush on Chrysler's meager funds. The banks smelled blood in the water and refused to fund credit lines and had begun calling loans. New debt was out of the question. Dealers resisted the extra deliveries that Chrysler had been pushing to improve sales numbers. The unions were panicked. All drawbridges were being raised in anticipation of the inevitable insolvency and bankruptcy.

At that time Chrysler transferred vehicles coming off the assembly line that weren't ordered by dealers into a "sales bank." The parking lots around its headquarters and assembly plants were filled with vehicles in the sales bank. Worse yet, production was substantially above real sales, which meant that costs were continuing at a high rate despite collapsing volume and revenue. These costs were not visible on the income statement because they were embedded in the ballooning inventories and dealer receivables. Chrysler's decline was in the headlines virtually every day.

Getting the facts right and uncovering and facing hard truths are always the first steps toward solving a problem.

Without the government or a miracle, Chrysler was going down. Chrysler put all its chips on government assistance. Iacocca believed that bankruptcy would result in liquidation. He argued that people would stop buying cars from a firm that couldn't guarantee service, and its cars would lose their resale value. The liquidity crisis could not be solved without additional funds, and no commercial lenders were willing to offer credit to the company. Booz Allen and Salomon were focused on whether the company could avoid bankruptcy/liquidation and successfully reorganize if the government provided bridge financing for the turnaround. A breakup and sale of the company were off the table.

Jerry Greenwald had been assigned as principal liaison between Chrysler and our two firms, Booz Allen and Salomon. Greenwald had been hired by Iacocca from Ford Venezuela shortly before as Chrysler's vice president and controller. Greenwald in turn hired his chief financial officer at Ford Venezuela, Steve Miller, as assistant treasurer. We met with Greenwald daily. Wolfensohn, Greenwald, and I worked closely together for almost two years.

Our view was that Chrysler had several outstanding people. Iacocca was probably the best top executive in the industry. He had been hired a year earlier to be Riccardo's successor and had already begun to strengthen Chrysler's management team with several current and retired Ford executives. Hal Sperlick, who preceded Iacocca from Ford to Chrysler, was one of the best product planners in the business. John Day was an outstanding executive who had run Chrysler Europe successfully and was now in charge of defense and other non-automotive businesses. I knew Day previously in Paris. Greenwald, Miller, and several of the other former Ford people were exceptional—there was a nucleus of management talent—but most were relatively new in their positions. Chrysler was, nevertheless, overwhelmed by the economic/oil crisis, the impact of regulations, and countless management mistakes of the past. When you lose customer confidence, the fall can be sudden and fatal.

Business is people. People cause problems. People solve problems.

We met with Riccardo and Iacocca separately. Riccardo was in shock and virtually unable to discuss solutions. Iacocca gave us a polite hearing but was unwilling to show his hand beyond advocating government help. Iacocca had been head of the Ford Division. I was at Ford thirteen years earlier and ten levels below Iacocca. I knew him by reputation only, but enough to know that he was Chrysler's best hope for survival.

At the end of the three-week period, Booz Allen and Salomon had a meeting with the top management and Dick Dilworth to discuss findings and conclusions. Gutfreund of Salomon concluded that it would be very difficult for Chrysler to survive but didn't shut the door. We reviewed our findings and conclusions, adding that in our view the only way Chrysler could survive was to take draconian measures immediately to cut costs and raise cash, including selling the profitable defense business, reducing the product platforms from three car lines to two, undertaking a major restructuring of the organization, cutting break-even volume in half and reducing the staff by at least 25 percent, aligning production with sales—and securing major financial support.

We added that they needed double the amount of financial assistance from Congress that had originally been estimated—$1.5 billion rather than $750 million. We had met with Jim Blanchard, the congressman from Chrysler's district who was leading the effort in Congress for the Chrysler bailout, and had his support for the higher number. His advice: "Ask for all you might need because there will be no second bite at the apple."

Riccardo sat silently. Iacocca erupted. I can't remember his words, but his message was crystal clear: No way in hell would Chrysler make the changes we recommended. Dilworth somehow saw a little light at the end of the disastrous tunnel and suggested a meeting with Treasury.

A week later the Treasury Secretary's office called a meeting. Jim Farley and I were joined by three other partners. The conference room was grand, even stately, with large chandeliers, a twenty-five-foot ceiling decorated with murals, and several serious statues standing guard. Seating was set up around a large rectangle of tables with space in the center.

The Treasury team was on one long side of the rectangle with the secretary in the middle. Chrysler's board and half a dozen top managers sat across the divide, with John Riccardo in the middle flanked by Iacocca and Dilworth. Booz Allen and Salomon had one short side of the rectangle and a group of silent but diligent analysts occupied the fourth. I was never sure who they were but was positive they weren't press or media. It was made clear in advance that press would not be allowed. As we saw when we arrived, the mob of journalists at the main entrance had discovered our secret Saturday morning meeting.

Secretary Miller opened by thanking everyone for coming on short notice and explained that the President was very concerned about the failing condition of Chrysler and the impact its bankruptcy could have on the economy. He stated that the purpose of the meeting was to discuss the plan for Chrysler's turnaround and whether government assistance was appropriate. Short and to the point. He then asked, "Who will be presenting the plan?" Riccardo was silent. Iacocca was silent. After a few awkward moments, Dilworth offered that he would.

The report was the presentation we delivered to management a week before, which, of course, did not have management's endorsement. Dilworth was in a terrible spot. He was not an automotive guy and certainly was not prepared to deliver the report. After several painful minutes, Secretary Miller interrupted with: "OK, I think we have the gist of it. What do your consultants have to say?"

John Gutfreund spoke up. Gutfreund was a legend on Wall Street. He had a tough, take-no-prisoners attitude and was a brilliant bond trader. He ran one of the top investment-banking firms in the world with an iron fist. He kicked off by saying that Chrysler didn't have a chance and closed by saying the government should not risk any taxpayer money on the company. In less than ten minutes, Gutfreund appeared to have trashed any hope of government help for Chrysler.

I couldn't read the Secretary's reaction. He was stone-faced, and his team followed his lead. The Chrysler side of the room looked like Detroit had just lost the World Series in the final inning. They were deflated and depressed. No one had known what Salomon was going to recommend. I was astonished more by Gutfreund's vehemence than his message. The Secretary simply said, "And Booz Allen, what is your opinion?"

My turn. Farley wished me luck. I started by describing the dire situation in vivid color. I did not attempt to deliver our report to management. Rather, I said there was a solution, but it was draconian. I explained the recommendations we made to the management team and added that implementation would be difficult, and the risk of failure was high. After a short discussion, Secretary Miller concluded that Chrysler should work with Booz Allen to see if there could be an agreed approach to move forward. If so, the matter would be taken to Congress for appropriations. The meeting ended. I sincerely doubt that many decisions by our government are made that quickly and that crisply.

Dick Dilworth was ecstatic. He rushed over to say how happy he was and wanted us to start working that afternoon. He told me that the board had just fired Salomon Brothers.

I told him that we would be happy to work with Chrysler, but there were three conditions that we believed had to be met to ensure success. First, Iacocca should be elected CEO immediately. Second, Salomon should be rehired, with Wolfensohn as lead partner. Third, we needed to be hired by the company, not the board, and Iacocca needed to call and meet with me before we began. Dilworth agreed with all three and suggested that we start now. I repeated that we would start when all three conditions were met. I also explained why each was crucial to Chrysler's success. The company needed strong leadership urgently and Iacocca was the right man at the right time. Chrysler clearly needed an investment banker and Jim Wolfensohn was the perfect choice. And he had a different view of Chrysler's potential viability than his boss had.

That afternoon, the board elected Iacocca chairman and CEO and rehired Salomon Brothers. Dilworth called to tell me and added that Iacocca was fine with Booz Allen working with Chrysler. I repeated my final condition. I knew that Iacocca never used management consultants and viewed executives who did as unable to do their jobs themselves. If Iacocca "allowed" us to work with the company but let others know that we were only there because the government mandated it, we would have no impact.

Three weeks passed before Iacocca's office called me to set a meeting. During those three weeks, Dilworth called countless times telling me that Iacocca was ready for us to start and we should move ahead. I stuck to my position. The meeting occurred in Iacocca's home on a Saturday afternoon. It wasn't clear whether he didn't want to waste valuable time during the work week or he didn't want to be seen meeting with a consultant. Nevertheless, it was pleasant and remarkably productive. We even talked about his dislike of consultants.

In a negotiation, decide what is truly important to you and stick with it even if it means walking away.

Iacocca and I discussed our recommended actions to turn Chrysler around in some detail. We had little disagreement except regarding elimination of the third platform. He clearly wanted to continue to be a full-line car company. As cars were designed and manufactured at that time, each platform drove significant unique costs. My argument was that Chrysler didn't have the resources to compete across three platforms. Better to focus your limited resources on fewer products, at least for now. In fact, we discussed that near-term Chrysler should focus on one car line, a compact car, code named the "K-car," which was just about ready for production. I think he agreed, because he focused all Chrysler's efforts and resources on the small, front-wheel-drive, fuel-efficient K-car. Iacocca and Sperlick had wanted to build a car just like that at Ford but were turned down by Henry Ford II. Sperlick began working on the car when he joined Chrysler two years earlier. In any case, Chrysler's turnaround became a bet on the K-car. Later, the K-car platform was used for an entire range of new cars and minivans. Iacocca got his full line of cars, even without the platform he had dropped.

Over the following twenty-four months or so, we worked closely with Chrysler's top management team to get Congressional approval of the $1.5 billion loan guarantee program and implement the turnaround plan. Jerry Greenwald continued as Chrysler's point man. He was promoted to CFO and then to president and chief operating officer. Steve Miller managed the transformation of the capital structure and balance sheet and marshaled all the support teams to prepare and deliver the reams of documentation necessary for Congressional and bank approvals. Steve was elected treasurer of Chrysler. The amount and form of the government's support changed over the course of the approval process. In the end, Chrysler went with $1.5 billion in loans guaranteed by the U.S. government—better politically than tax credits and preferred by Iacocca. The loans carried warrants (owned by the government) for Chrysler common stock. Each tranche of loans had to be approved by a Loan Guarantee Board and required letters from Booz Allen and Salomon Brothers certifying that Chrysler was and would continue to be a viable enterprise. Our letters needed to include a projection of operating results for calendar years 1980 and 1981.

There was considerable drama around the preparation and submission of the letters. Iacocca always believed that our projections were far too conservative, and he let me know in graphically colorful language. As it turned out, our projections were close to the mark. Lee's optimism was legendary. He never let up. Two years later, Iacocca held a wonderful luncheon at the 21 Club in Manhattan for many of those who played roles in the turnaround. In his comments he chided me for being so conservative. I reminded him that we were right.

Chrysler was front-page news for two years as it teetered toward bankruptcy. I received as many as five calls daily from the press attempting to get inside information. I had learned how to keep my mouth shut when I served in the Naval Security Group, which was so top secret I couldn't even tell my father what I was doing.

Prior to government approval of the loan guarantees, there was a major debate in Congress and among business leaders about the appropriateness of a government bailout. There was also a debate about Chrysler's chance of survival even with a bailout; the overwhelming view in the media was "low to none." Our job was to determine whether and how Chrysler could survive, not whether a bailout was good public policy. It was the politicians' job to weigh the damage to the economy of Chrysler's failure versus creating an unsustainable policy precedent— the moral hazard argument. Nevertheless, I was comfortable with a solution that used the government's credit to give the company access to funds at normal commercial rates.

A few days before my testimony to Congress, I received a late-night call from Pete Peterson, then CEO of Lehman Brothers and former Secretary of Commerce, who was also about to testify. Peterson was joined on the call by Steve Schwarzman, his closest advisor. I knew Steve from an auto conference in Geneva. Their concern was the widely shared likelihood that Chrysler could not survive. Our two-hour discussion was excellent preparation for Congress because Peterson and Schwarzman thought more like Gutfreund. They were two savvy businessmen with very tough questions. I had been confident from the time of our meeting with the U.S. Treasury Department and that Saturday with Iacocca that the odds of success were high, and I told Peterson and Schwarzman so and why. I don't think I convinced them of Chrysler's ability to pull through, but I feel I got them to soften their positions at least.

Argue your side of any question based on the facts as you know them, but listen to all sides to deepen your fact base and understanding.

I appeared before the House Subcommittee on Economic Stabilization of the Committee of Banking, Finance, and Urban Affairs, which was handling the Chrysler matter. The room was large and crowded with the media. The Committee members sat on a raised platform. My colleagues and I sat at the "witness" table below—intentionally awkward, I am sure. After the Chair rambled for about five minutes, he called on me for my testimony. The Committee had two questions:

- Why should the government bail out Chrysler . . . or any corporation, for that matter?
- Could the company survive if given the requested loan guarantees and . . . why?

My testimony deferred on the first question and focused on viability. I described the dire situation, the recommended plan of cost reduction and restructuring and the economics of the auto industry. I told them that avoiding insolvency was only possible with the requested loan guarantees because the company was insolvent without credit and was frozen out of the credit markets. Many of the major actions in the plan were already being implemented. The new leadership team was in place, and if aggressive implementation continued along with concessions from unions, dealers, and suppliers, odds of success were high. Without any one of those elements, the company couldn't survive.

Each committee member grilled me, and it was obvious who was likely to vote for and against based on their attitudes, questions, and political party. We left thinking we did our best but unsure which way Congress would go.

I have reflected on the policy issues around government bailouts over the years and particularly during the financial meltdown of 2008 and 2009. My conclusion is that government assistance should be rare and only when a reorganization under bankruptcy protection or sale isn't possible and the domino effect of a failure would be truly catastrophic nationally or internationally.

Even then, there should be strict rules governing the process: First, the government should play no role in running the business. Second, the government should not intervene to favor one or another constituency. For example, there are laws in place that govern the disposition of assets and ownership and that should be upheld. Finally, the odds of success have to be high, and the deal has to be favorable to taxpayers—a good return for the risk they take. The government must be willing to give enough help to avoid the company returning to the well because the first round was inadequate.

The 1979 bailout of Chrysler met all of these criteria. The bailouts of the auto industry in 2008 and 2009 violated them all. For example, the bondholders were forced by the government to accept a major reduction in the value of their bonds without the contractual payment in stock. Stock was given to the unions, in effect a mandated transfer from the bondholders. And the government took over the management for a period of time. Finally, there was no benefit to the taxpayers for their risk . . . only to the unions and the politicians.

People, especially those in government, rarely take the right lessons from history when their interests are threatened.

Iacocca did a spectacular job of leading the company out of near bankruptcy. He got the unions to agree to a significant reduction in wages until the company was out of danger, not once but twice, with his personal commitment to return wages to market levels when the company was healthy again. They trusted him. He gained the cooperation of the dealers to take several actions to help the recovery. They trusted him. He worked with suppliers to continue deliveries without COD and with extended payment terms. They also trusted him.

Under the Chrysler Corporation Loan Guarantee Act, dealers and suppliers had to contribute at least $180 million in total concessions, and Iacocca persuaded them to do so. Finally, he and Miller got 100 percent of the banks to accept the restructuring of their loans as a condition of obtaining loan guarantees. Iacocca was the spirit in the company that swung its attitude from resignation to belief in the future. Investors, bondholders, and customers became believers also. Chrysler implemented every measure in our draconian plan because it became Iacocca's plan.

The Loan Guarantee Act was signed by President Carter in January 1980. The next three years were rocky for the entire auto industry because of a deep recession. The sword of bankruptcy hung over Chrysler. Nevertheless, almost immediately, sales rebounded, losses shrunk, and whole sections of offices in the headquarters emptied. The lots full of cars and trucks evaporated as production slowed and sales rose. The K-car was a great success in the market. The defense and non-automotive businesses were sold along with Rootes and Simca, the Chrysler auto subsidiaries in the U.K. and France, giving Chrysler necessary capital. The Mighty Ship Chrysler was turning around. Chrysler turned profitable in mid-1982 and had record profits in 1983.

Chrysler repaid 100 percent of its guaranteed loans with interest in August 1983, seven years ahead of schedule. Taxpayers earned an estimated $311 million on the warrants. As an investor, the government did very well with Chrysler.

Many of the people who played key roles in the turnaround went on to very successful careers. Jim Wolfensohn set up his own investment counseling firm, Wolfensohn & Co., with Paul Volcker, the former chair of the Federal Reserve, and later served for ten years as president of the

World Bank. Jerry Greenwald became president of Chrysler and later chairman and CEO of United Airlines. John Day became chairman and CEO of Bendix Corp. Steve Miller became a leading turnaround specialist as chairman at a succession of high-profile rescues, including Bethlehem Steel, Federal Mogul, Delphi Corp., and AIG. Several members of the Booz Allen team launched a successful global automotive practice for the firm. Pete Peterson and Steve Schwarzman founded the Blackstone Group in 1985, which became the most successful new Wall Street firm in decades. Lee Iacocca retired from Chrysler in 1992 and became an iconic statesman in the business world and at one point was pressured to run for President of the United States. He declined.

POSTSCRIPT

Chrysler had flourished in the 1980s and built up a strong cash position. In 1995 billionaire Kirk Kerkorian attempted greenmail and eventually a hostile takeover of Chrysler, but the effort failed. Kerkorian was demanding that Chrysler buy back stock or declare a large cash dividend with most of the $12 billion it held in cash. We were asked by Bob Eaton, then CEO of Chrysler, to analyze how much cash Chrysler should retain on its balance sheet. At the conclusion of our study, my response was, "far more than Chrysler presently holds." Chrysler had been close to insolvent during every recession since World War II. It was easy for us to demonstrate that it would likely happen again unless they had a very large cash cushion. Eaton refused Kerkorian's request, triggering the attempted takeover.

A few years later, Daimler-Benz merged with Chrysler to form DaimlerChrysler. The merger broke up in 2007 as Chrysler results faltered. Chrysler filed for bankruptcy in 2009 during the financial crisis and was bailed out by the Obama administration. The government engineered an alliance between Chrysler and Fiat, with Fiat taking a strong minority position in Chrysler.

In 2014 Fiat North America completed its acquisition of the Chrysler Group. Analysts agree Fiat did extremely well on the deal. Chrysler's value at the time was placed at $10.4 billion; Fiat paid $6.3 billion. The U.S. taxpayers, bondholders, and stockholders didn't do so well.

The Chrysler story was typical of many manufacturing companies. Success is driven by creating products consumers want and by delivering value in price, quality, performance, and reliability with a competitive cost structure. Failures can almost always be traced to inability to achieve those objectives. Chrysler did it well for over a decade under Iacocca. Though there were bumps in the road, the company grew and strengthened financially. The failed merger with Daimler and the 2008–2009 recessions were the end of Chrysler's independence. Nevertheless, the company had nearly three decades of renewed success, a time when it drove innovation in the American automobile industry with products such as the K-car and created an entirely new segment of family transportation with the revolutionary minivan.

The Chrysler experience in 1979–1981 was for me a stellar example of what a consultant actually does. Business at the top level is as compelling, challenging, and satisfying a career as there can be.

Chapter Two

WE ALL START AT THE BOTTOM

O f course, I didn't step into the Chrysler boardroom without three decades of education, business experience, and life lessons to help guide me. Where you come from and how you prepare for the future are crucial to where you go. This foundation consists of three major elements: education, character, and discipline. You need them all. Here's my story of the building of my foundation and what I learned along the way.

EARLY JOBS

My first job was delivering the *Herald American,* one of two afternoon daily newspapers in Chicago. I was about eight when my brother, Jere, recruited me to help on his route. Ironically, the first and last jobs in my career were with Chicago newspapers—from delivery boy at the *Herald American* to CEO/publisher at the *Sun-Times*—interesting career bookends. There's no telling where your career will take you when you are eight years old.

Jere and I worked for the post office delivering mail during the Christmas holidays. It may have been the highest-paying job in my life based on pay received for effort, productivity, and hours worked. An early lesson: The government spends too much to achieve too little, which is still true today.

My next part-time job was less notable and much less successful—door-to-door sales of some kind of salve that promised life-altering changes at ten cents a tin. It was a dismal failure—only one customer, my mother, despite days knocking on all neighbors' doors. Scratch door-to-door selling from my career aspiration list.

Learning what you don't want to do is almost as important as learning what you do want to do.

Jere and I started caddying at Beverly Country Club, our first summer jobs. What a deal—carrying a golf bag for eighteen holes in beautiful weather, getting paid $1.97 plus tip and playing golf for free on Mondays on one of the top courses in Chicago. (Beverly Country Club became the home of the Western Open, one of the most important professional tournaments at that time.) By the end of my third summer, I was getting the best players and the good tippers and watched Sam Snead (he had the most beautiful swing in the world) play my favorite course with Tony and Charlie Penna. Tony was a tour pro, and brother Charlie was the club pro at Beverly Country Club. Caddying is great for young kids—it teaches golf, good behavior, discipline, and how to keep your eye on the ball. While waiting for "loops" we played "hoops" (basketball) with boys I would see again on opposing high school teams. My first and only hole-in-one occurred on the 12th at Beverly at age thirteen.

Golf would be an interesting career, but you would have to beat guys like Sam Snead, Jack Nicklaus, and Tiger Woods. Be ambitious but realistic.

Next came my first management job, at a hot dog hut on North Avenue, Chicago's best beach. Jere worked in the main restaurant a half mile away. I was alone, which made me the manager. The owner was shrewd. On the first day, he told me to eat all the hot dogs I wanted for free but to pay for ice cream and Cokes. By the end of the week, I never wanted to eat another hot dog, ever.

Know both the strengths and weaknesses of those you manage and leverage them.

The hours were 10 A.M. to 5 P.M.; the weather was beautiful, as were many of the girls on the beach. What's not to like? If you can find a summer job like that at age fifteen, take it.

My final high school summer job was at Acorn Wire & Iron Works. My father knew the owner and thought something more like real work would be good for me. Acorn was a small company in Chicago, which cut, shaped, and distributed iron bar products. I was on the floor stocking things and in the shipping room. The work was heavy, dirty, and noisy. One guy took me under his wing. He was from the South Side and said, "You have to learn to protect yourself." He taught me about knives and coached me in back of the plant to whip out the knife, flip the blade open, and stab the trademark on a cardboard box. I flunked every part of the test, particularly the speed. He said I'd be toast without big improvement. My mother wasn't thrilled about my self-defense training. My lesson: Rely on my wits in life rather than attempt to match skills with knife slingers.

Every Thanksgiving and Christmas holiday, our father bundled us up (it was always cold in Chicago) and took us for several days to Cougle Commission Company, the Freidheim family-owned business going back to our grandfather, Louis Edgar Freidheim. They bought poultry from farms, slaughtered and dressed them, and sold them to restaurants, hotels, and small grocery stores. Dad, Jere, and I helped our Uncle Edgar with the holiday spike in the turkey business. It was cold, messy, unpleasant work with modest pay, which we were not worth. The big plus was lunches at Barney's, an iconic restaurant frequented by Irish politicians—lively atmosphere, good food, and warm. My cousin and Edgar's son, Lee, and his kids still own and run Cougle—but no more cutting chickens' heads off. These days it is one of the largest private companies processing and distributing poultry in the midwest.

My summer and part-time jobs were time valuably spent. It was my introduction to the next fifty years of my career.

The most important lessons from those jobs—reliability, getting to work on time, learning your job, putting in the required hours, working hard and achieving what was required, earning a paycheck regardless of how small, following direction, and figuring out how to get things done—might seem obvious, but they will put you ahead of 95 percent of your peers.

I learned later that not every kid had that opportunity. In fact, few did then, and even now. What a huge advantage. These were the basic disciplines necessary in any job. I also began to be aware of different management styles and what was good or bad about them. I learned what I didn't want to do. It was crystal clear that the better educated you are, the broader and more interesting the options for your career. And from a very early age, I understood that I would have a family and be responsible for taking care of them, which meant working and earning enough money. It was scary but clear.

Do everything you can to get summer jobs for yourself (as a kid), your children, your grandchildren, and as many other kids as you can.

Like most kids, sports were more important to me than studies. When it was time to choose a high school, my preference was clear—go where the best sports teams were. My mom and dad wanted me to go to St. Ignatius College Prep, which had the best record of placing students in good colleges but a horrible record in sports, except cross-country running which was of no interest. In retrospect, this is one argument I am glad to have lost. St. Ignatius gave me superb training in discipline, how to study and learn, and character. It had a major impact on my life. Incidentally, in my senior year, our basketball team finished third in the city, well ahead of the schools I would have chosen.

Parents have responsibility for their children—their safety, education, health, and character—for at least sixteen years, more in most cases. Listen carefully to them. Their judgment of what's best for you is likely better than yours during that time.

Life is a ladder—you start at the bottom and imagine your dreams at the top. Your first big challenge is your education. How well you do in each year and each segment of your education determines the options you have for the next step in your life. The better you perform, the greater your opportunities. You go through each segment one rung at a time, careful not to miss a rung because the next one becomes *so much* harder.

NOTRE DAME

Deciding whether to go to college is a life-altering moment. Deciding which college to attend and your major are important but not life-altering. My decision whether to go to college was made before I was born and never appeared to be an option, thanks to my parents. Lucky me.

Translate the values you wish your children to adopt into expectations. This works much better than rules or lectures.

Notre Dame was my mom's family school—her two brothers attended and family legend held that her great-uncle was the architect of the Basilica at Notre Dame and a few residence halls. My older brother, Jere, also went there. My mother played the *Notre Dame Victory March* on our piano every morning before breakfast. I succumbed to the pressure.

I chose chemical engineering as my major. The choice was not the product of exhaustive research or penetrating analysis of my skills and interests. Someone had told me there was a shortage of engineers and I liked my one chemistry course in high school. This was a good lesson how *not* to make an important decision.

I concluded after my first chemical engineering lab course that I would never become a chemical engineer. Why, oh why, didn't I switch majors? Inertia is a powerful force. Also something inside made me feel that once you start something, you should finish it. In retrospect a bad idea. With 20/20 hindsight, I should have taken a liberal arts program with a math or economics major. If I had had a knowledgeable mentor at the time, he or she probably would have guided me to switch. Fortunately, I picked up a liberal arts education during my four years with the Navy through an extensive reading program, the Navy's language school, and traveling/living abroad. More important, Notre Dame was the perfect place for my character formation and discipline. I owe a lot to Notre Dame.

Notre Dame has always been considered a "special place." Tough rules set the boundaries, and expectations gave academics their rightful place in student life. The spiritual life and the spirit of Notre Dame raise it to its special place. Its "spirit," however, is what made Notre Dame a unique university—somewhat like the Marine Corps' spirit, intangible but real. Football and Knute Rockne are probably credited too much.

The founder, a missionary priest from France, Father Edward Sorin, built a Catholic college in the middle of nowhere in 1842 with little but his vision and the help of a small band of followers. When the main building burned to the ground in 1879, Father Sorin stood tall. Rather than folding his cassock and returning to France, Father Sorin declared: "My dreams for Notre Dame were too small and we will rebuild a much bigger, grander university that will become one of the greatest in the world." Sorin's round two would include a golden dome (covered in real gold leaf) with a statue of Mary on top. Rockne, a non-Catholic until shortly before the plane crash that took his life, rode that spirit onto the football field, creating legends that still inspire young athletes across America.

In choosing a college, consider the three most important elements of your education: intellectual, preparation for your career, and character development.

CHOOSING A CAREER

Most people "find their careers" by accident, inertia, or doing what their parents did. But the choice of a career is far too important just to let it happen. "What will I be when I grow up?" is an important question for everyone and deserves more thought and research than 99 percent of the human race gives it. This is not a pitch for reading books on careers, but rather for how to think about that question. My sources are my experience and my mistakes.

My summer jobs growing up did more to convince me what I didn't want in my career than to cast light on what interested me. Most importantly, they convinced me that school should be taken seriously. It also became clear that the correct direction should capitalize on my strengths and interests and even excite me, and avoid my weaknesses. I knew nothing about business and little about most other career options.

During my final semester at Notre Dame, I signed up for a seminar with Professor Rich, dean of the College of Chemical Engineering. I liked the dean, and it sounded like an interesting softball course. The seminar turned out to have nothing to do with engineering. Rather it was about how companies in the chemical industry were structured and operated. One of the principal examples was Christiana Securities, which was an investment company established in 1919 by a wing of the DuPont family to consolidate their stock into a control position of DuPont de Nemours—the chemical company everyone knows as DuPont. They also used it to purchase major stakes in other large companies like General Motors (25 percent). Through this holding company, they could control corporations without being majority shareholders. I was intrigued.

Nothing in my work experience or school opened my imagination like that course. While chemical engineering was not right for me, business rang my bell. My next steps seemed clear—three years in the Navy and then business school, Harvard Business School, of course. At that time HBS was the undisputed leader of a small but growing number of graduate business schools. It was the beginning of the business school boom. HBS graduates referred to it as *the* business school, arrogantly assuming that there was only one. With equal arrogance, I assumed that getting in would be no problem and did no research for a backup.

We were in the middle of interview season for jobs after graduation. I had the commitment to the Navy in return for my NROTC scholarship, but interviewed anyway. I could see what kinds of jobs were out there for ChemEs; and it might be wise to have a job lined up when leaving the Navy. The job market in 1957 was fantastic, particularly for engineers. Lots of companies came to campus, and everyone in our ChemE class got offers. As was to be expected, most of the offers were in chemical plants as engineers, which had no interest for me. During my interview with Procter & Gamble in Cincinnati after visiting a soap plant, I asked about other possibilities. They gave me a blank stare that seemed to say, "Chemical engineers go to soap plants." At lunch in the P&G management cafeteria, a special table was reserved for the top executives. I stared at those executives for most of the lunch, imagining being among them some day.

One company, Glidden Paint, was looking for people in sales. It was a leader in its industry, and the recruiter made selling paint sound interesting—and lucrative. It sure would be better than a soap or paint plant. We made a mutual commitment for me to begin work three years later. When I contacted Glidden in the spring of 1961 while cycling out of the Navy, it was clear they had totally forgotten about me. It was just as well. Everything since graduation confirmed that I wanted to be a businessman, not a plant engineer or paint salesman.

While in the Navy, I gave myself a liberal arts education. This step was important to my belief that a career in business was right for me. I had to learn much more about the world and people than I had in chemical engineering. The Navy sent me to their Russian language school. Travel, language, books on history, and literature expanded my thinking about the world, about people, and about myself. Nineteenth-century Russia likely has some of the greatest literature in history. I was intellectually ready for business school.

CARNEGIE BUSINESS SCHOOL

While I was stationed in Turkey, the Navy gave me a special assignment with the commander of the 6th Fleet in Villefranche-sur-Mer on the French Riviera in the summer of 1960. We were anchored in the harbor and had plenty of time off. Unbelievable duty. We pulled up anchor once that summer—to sail to Rome for the 1960 summer Olympics. I became a regular at the Monte Carlo Golf Club, overlooking the Principality of Monaco. One day I showed up at the first tee and was paired with a friendly American. Bob Trueblood was a senior partner of Touche Ross Bailey & Smart, one of the then Big Eight public accounting firms. He was leading Touche Ross's entry into management consulting. He was also a visiting professor at the new business school at Carnegie Institute of Technology (now known as Carnegie-Mellon University).

We had lunch after golf in Eze, a walled village carved in a mountainside by the Romans two thousand years ago. The restaurant, Le Chèvre d'Or, sits on a cliff 1,200 feet above Monte Carlo and must have the most beautiful view of any restaurant in the world. Trueblood made a compelling case for me to consider Carnegie and consulting.

The Graduate School for Industrial Administration (GSIA) was founded on the premise that information technology would become a major driver of businesses. Virtually all the students were engineering, math, and science majors in college. Classes were small, and the faculty was off-the-charts brilliant and well ahead of everyone on computers and artificial intelligence, which Carnegie and Trueblood believed would play a central role in business in the future. It seems like an obvious prediction now, but not in 1960 when computers were in their infancy. Trueblood was aggressively moving Touche Ross and the accounting profession in that direction, and Carnegie was the research hub. I was all in.

It sounded good enough for me to apply to Carnegie in addition to my first (and more obvious) choice, Harvard. HBS accepted me but claimed my father wasn't poor enough for me to receive financial aid—though I knew he had to support Jere in medical school and three more through college. Carnegie offered me a full-tuition scholarship and an assistantship job. My savings would not have covered my first semester, so I chose Carnegie's GSIA. Who knows what my life would have been if my choice had been Harvard?

My accidental golf partner in Monte Carlo, Bob Trueblood, became chair and CEO of Touche Ross and president of the AICPA and changed the accounting profession. Touche Ross became a leader in management consulting in financial systems and information technology.

Interestingly, Herb Simon, the father of artificial intelligence and Nobel Laureate in economics, was the board chair of the management game team at Carnegie of which I was president. What an experience!

Nine Nobel Prize winners have come out of that business school, most in the 1960s. Three were on the faculty in 1960—Merton Miller, Franco Modigliani, and Herb Simon; two more were classmates of mine—Ollie Williamson and Dale Mortensen; and one more, Bob Lucas, joined the faculty in 1963, my final year there. Other professors like Bill Cooper and Jim March became legends in the information technology revolution, and Dick Cyert, my microeconomics professor, became president of the university. Allan Meltzer taught me economics, and I met with him a number of times over the years. He passed away in May 2017 while still on the faculty. Allan should have won his Nobel Prize years ago. Interestingly, his last book, which was published in 2008, was *Why Capitalism?*, one of my bibles. Together, this group was comparable to the collection of scientists on the Manhattan Project during World War II.

In addition to a terrific education for the business world of the future, I was blessed with a few outstanding mentors. My assistantship involved working with a professor each year. In my first year, Hal Leavitt was my professor. His specialty was management psychology. He focused on how organizations functioned and knew a lot about specific companies. We discussed several professions and companies our grads pursued. Two opportunities struck me as really interesting: consulting and corporate finance. Consulting appeared a perfect fit for a Gemini, which I am: a constant diet of tough problems in different situations, great exposure and responsibility at an early age, and independence. The downside was also obvious: extensive travel. Leavitt briefed me on the best firms, which he thought were equal—Booz Allen Hamilton and McKinsey.

But he thought the personality of Booz Allen was a better fit for me—a sink-or-swim culture that rewarded performance over style and a hard analytical edge. McKinsey prided itself more on pedigree, and had a more controlled environment. Both enjoyed outstanding reputations, and both hired my classmates. My assessment of the people they hired matched Leavitt's description of the firms. This wisdom was stashed away in the back of my mind, though I was unaware of how important it would become.

Leavitt introduced our class to Olin Larson, a mythical character in a book about a young GSIA grad on the finance staff of the Ford Motor Company. The book was a research project to teach us how to be successful in the early years of our careers. Larson was perfect, he did everything right. But he did nothing spectacular and was low-key—not how most of us figured we should operate in the competitive shark tank we were about to enter. Larson used his analytical skills but hid them as a soft-spoken person more interested in understanding what the company, his boss, and boss's boss needed than demonstrating his wizardry in operation research. I loved the model and needed a big dose of it to control my urge to demonstrate my IQ, whatever it was.

The book was written about an actual graduate four or five years earlier, who had a meteoric rise among Ford's fabled finance staff. His name was Bill Sick. At that time Ford had a reputation for attracting the best and brightest from the top business schools. It was viewed as the "academy" for the best in corporate finance in the country. You could jump from there to top operating jobs at Ford—most of the top executives then and for years after came from the finance staff—or you could be hired away to become a top financial executive at other companies. I interviewed with Ford, loved it, and joined under the condition that they would start me in Bill Sick's department. They agreed and paid me $9,000 per year, 50 percent above the median household income in the early 1960s. We were rich! More important, this career track appeared to be right for me. The work would demand the best of my analytical skills. I would work with smart, talented people and learn a lot. The industry was very interesting. The company was successful. And options to move up or move out were attractive. It had taken six years since graduation from Notre Dame to get my first career job, but it was time well spent and would be worth the journey if I had found the right place.

FORD MOTOR COMPANY

Ford turned out to be a master class in financial planning and control, but not the ultimate right place for me. Nevertheless, it was an excellent step on my career ladder. After two years, the process was becoming repetitive. One or two jumps upward would be more of the same, though managing rather than doing the analyses. After some soul-searching, I concluded that the only jobs in finance that were really interesting were many years away and far from certain. Time to explore other options.

Changing companies or career paths is an important decision. Make sure you are doing it for the right reason. But don't be afraid to explore other options.

Many of my colleagues had moved from finance to Ford's product development, marketing, sales, and manufacturing, including Bill Sick, who had become a plant manager. Sick agreed it was too early for me to move directly into a meaningful management role. Manufacturing at Ford was not for me—I could hear through the shared wall in my office with the vice president of manufacturing as he shouted expletives at his top managers for five minutes before slamming down the phone—not a good prospect for my future. More on Ford in the next chapter.

I spent the better part of a year searching for my next career step. The economy and job market in the mid-sixties were strong so I had a number of opportunities.

BOOZ ALLEN & HAMILTON

About this time, Paul Anderson, a classmate and good friend from Carnegie, called. His company, Booz Allen Hamilton, was looking for people like me in the Chicago office. Two visits and a heart-to-heart conversation with Paul convinced me that consulting and Booz Allen were a good fit for me.

My description of management consulting—to myself and later to recruits: You are handed a problem (1) that the management team hasn't been able to or hasn't the resources to figure out; (2) that is important enough for the company to pay an outside firm to help decide what to do; (3) in an industry and company about which the CEO and his team know tons more than you do; and (4) you have three months to come up with the answer and convince the client to accept and act on it. For the right person, this is the most exciting, invigorating, stimulating environment imaginable. For the wrong person, it is pure hell.

Consulting was excellent training for top corporate management. The experience and exposure to a range of industries and companies broadened my knowledge of business. Working with management and boards improved my interpersonal skills, did wonders for my self-confidence, and launched an excellent network of relationships.

My reaction to the partners and staff was very positive. I met top-quality people with serious knowledge and broad experience, in a meritocracy with a collaborative culture. The biggest question was travel. I had spent virtually every night at home since getting married. Consulting meant working where the clients were. My wife, Mitzi, and I discussed the pluses and minuses of consulting and Booz Allen and jointly concluded that it was worth a try . . . *for a year*. Even a short stint in consulting would be good for my career. Chicago was a big plus, given both our families were there and we now had three little ones for the grandparents to dote on.

Within a month at Booz Allen, I knew that it was a good place for me. Almost thirty-six years later, I retired as vice-chairman of the firm.

It took nine years after college to "find my career." I consider myself lucky because many (most?) people never find the right place. Either they stay put even when unhappy or they search forever, making bad choices throughout their working lives. Work is a large part of our time on this planet, and we owe it to ourselves and our families to have careers that provide a satisfying, challenging, rewarding life. You gotta love what you are doing.

The three indispensable steps in finding your career are:

1. Build a strong educational foundation that will open opportunities for a fulfilling career.
2. "What will I be when I grow up?" should be the product of a thoughtful journey of truly understanding yourself and seeking opportunities that are best for you, not the result of inertia or accident or a bigger paycheck. You should be in the driver's seat.
3. Seek counsel from trusted advisors and always keep an open mind to opportunities that knock on your door. Finding your career is a lifelong pursuit.

The early years of my professional career were focused on broadening my career horizons. Some people find their careers much earlier—Mozart was seven. Remember, a career lasts a lifetime and can have many chapters. Opportunities and challenges have continued to come my way for twenty years past normal retirement age. Throughout the process of "finding my career," I learned that good mentors are invaluable.

MENTORS

I have been fortunate to have had several mentors at crucial points in my life and career. During my school years, my parents were my primary mentors, along with a few priests who became good friends and advisors. At Carnegie, Hal Leavitt and Leland Hazzard, my professors, became valued mentors. Bill Sick and Allen Gilmore (my third boss at Ford and subsequently vice-chair of Ford) were my mentors at Ford. I was fortunate to have many mentors at Booz Allen—most notably Jim Allen, John Rhodes, and Jim Farley. In the Chicago community there were several more—particularly Don Perkins, Don Clark, and John Richman. All of these men gave me important counsel on my career and life. All were objective and willing to tell me what was in my best interest, even if I disagreed. All were trusted friends. Many more people helped and guided me along the way. Stan Druckenmiller, a very successful investor, said, "If you have to choose between a good mentor and more pay in a job, pick the mentor every time. In the long run you will be richer." Druckenmiller credits his extraordinary success to a few mentors.

Virtually every occupation is a trade—from brick layer to lawyer, from plumber to programmer, from electrician to executive, from mother to musician. Investors, priests, artists, golfers, coaches, scientists, educators, journalists, all are tradespeople at heart. You learn a trade by studying under a master. Think of a mentor as your master craftsman. For thousands of years, people became experts in their craft by working with a master of that craft. It's really not that different today, even though we have much more sophisticated tools to teach us fundamentals and techniques. The best performers in every field can point to a few mentors who helped them become the best. Even Da Vinci and Michelangelo had mentors.

And you should become a mentor of people whom you believe have promise and can benefit from your counsel. The relationship benefits both mentor and apprentice—the mentor has a vested interest in the apprentice's success, and the apprentice develops loyalty to the mentor. Both share the satisfaction of success.

Seek mentors at every stage in your life and select them carefully. Remember that "finding your career" is a lifetime pursuit.

FINDING MY LIFE PARTNER

Probably the most important decision for my career and my life was selecting the right life partner. No decision impacts your happiness, your success, your health more than your spouse. Most people make that decision early in their adult lives . . . and often for the wrong reasons and without the serious thought it deserves. I'm not going to say that my selection process was perfect, but the result was as close to perfect as possible in our unpredictable life. Together, Mitzi and I have created a great family and have shared a wonderful life. The story is told for our grandchildren in *Notes from Grampa*.

Take the time necessary to make the most important decision of your life. Determine in advance what is most important to you, and don't compromise on principles.

Chapter Three

CARS! CARS! CARS!

My job at Ford Motor Company and the Chrysler rescue project were part of my automotive story, but my involvement in the industry spanned much of my career. At Booz Allen I always relished the opportunity to work with carmakers. I found the auto industry to be a fascinating classroom for understanding how business works. Most of the lessons I learned with the auto industry have been applicable to many other industries. In addition, the history of this industry tracks the evolution of the economies of the developed world— and has been a major factor in the economic separation of the developed and developing nations. It's worth spending some time on cars.

THE CAR: A HISTORICAL PERSPECTIVE

The automobile is the ultimate consumer product. A car is the second-most-expensive purchase most individuals make, after their houses. Ever since the automobile was created, there has been a proliferation of models, features, colors, styles, powertrains, and price points to attract consumers. As the car grew in popularity, auto companies targeted their products to more and more refined market segments. The car has come to capture the personality, aspirations, behavior, and cultural class of its owners. The industry has become the model for consumer marketing and segmentation, which drives product design for virtually all consumer products. I received my consumer-product education in the auto industry.

Cars are synonymous with American ingenuity and discipline. The automobile made its debut late in the nineteenth century as a toy for the rich. Henry Ford saw an opportunity to put the masses on wheels by producing a cheap car. After several failures, Ford developed the Model T, and the auto industry took off.

Ford introduced the assembly line in 1913, an idea used elsewhere, which Ford thought was perfect for autos. Large personnel turnover resulted from the boredom of the assembly line. Ford solved the problem by raising the workers' pay to $5 a day, about double the then competitive wage. His logic: If the car was for the masses, the masses had to be able to afford to buy it. The Model T Ford was designed for the masses and was produced from 1908 to 1927 with few changes and only in black. Over twenty million were sold. Ford had over half the total U.S. car market by 1922, and almost all of the low-cost, mass segment, when competitors recognized the broad appeal of autos and came pouring into Ford's market.

The industry has long been a leader in innovation in manufacturing, starting with Ford's assembly line. From the 1930s through the 1960s most of these innovations came through the United States. U.S. engineering and manufacturing techniques were the best. The Japanese made extraordinary advances in efficiency and quality in the 1970s through the 1990s—good examples are *kanban,* the Japanese word for just-in-time inventory control, and worker-led quality control. Any worker can stop the assembly line if he sees a quality defect in a car. The auto industry was the first to adopt rigorous use of statistical controls and became the laboratory for efficient production for most manufacturing industries. I received my indoctrination in efficient production in the auto industry.

Ford changed transportation from horses to cars in the U.S. and eventually around the world. In many ways Henry Ford created the foundation for America's spectacular rise as an industrial giant and can justly be credited with launching America's mighty middle class. At the same time, a number of entrepreneurs were developing cars to suit the growing demand and changing tastes of American car buyers. In 1908, William Durant formed General Motors, a holding company for the Buick marque, and proceeded to buy thirty other auto companies, including Oldsmobile, Cadillac, and Oakland (predecessor to Pontiac), as well as parts manufacturers. In fact, Durant tried to buy Ford, but the bank reportedly balked at the loan. In 1924 Walter Chrysler bought the Maxwell Motor Corp. and changed the name of its car and company to Chrysler. Chrysler created two new brands, Plymouth and DeSoto, at different price points, and then purchased Dodge from the Dodge brothers. While the Model T sales continued through 1927, its dominance and market share fell.

Market leadership is not hereditary but instead must be earned continually.

New products captured the minds and wallets of American buyers. By the mid-1930s Ford had dropped to number three, behind GM and Chrysler, and was facing bankruptcy (not for the last time). Henry Ford had bought out his investors in 1919 and was on his own. GM, 25 percent owned by DuPont through Christiana Securities and backed by J.P. Morgan, had real financial muscle. Ford reorganized under bankruptcy twice, partly because of the Depression.

By 1935, the large majority of the U.S. auto industry had consolidated into three companies: General Motors, Ford, and Chrysler. All three manufactured most of their own engines and parts. Ford even produced its own steel. Their factories in the United States, like their European counterparts, were expropriated by the government between

1941 and 1945 for armament production for the war. The late 1940s were spent retooling and restarting production with models much like their pre-war predecessors.

The industry took off again in the late 1940s and sailed through the 1950s creating a blizzard of newly designed cars and trucks. My first car was a 1957 Ford Fairlane convertible—super hot!

Two titans led GM and Ford—Alfred P. Sloan, CEO at General Motors from the mid-1920s through the mid-1950s, and Henry Ford from the turn of the century until his death in 1947. Sloan is credited with initiating modern management principles—such as organizing around profit centers, applying financial controls to profit centers, and planned obsolescence through annual product changes. His principles are documented in his book *My Years at General Motors,* which became required reading at all business schools. His ideas were implemented widely in America. Throughout my consulting career, I kept those principles in my tool kit.

Henry Ford was best known for his early dramatic moves that put Ford well in front of his competition. But he failed to understand the evolving competitive environment and fell behind in the mid-1920s. Ford emerged from World War II virtually bankrupt. Henry Ford planned for his son, Edsel, to be his successor and made him president of the company in 1919. But Edsel died in 1943, forcing Ford back to running the company. Henry Ford died four years later at eighty-three with the company on the ropes.

Ten men who worked together on statistical analysis in the Air Force were recruited to Ford by its new, young president, Edsel's son Henry Ford II, to help Ford return to producing automobiles and profitability. The Whiz Kids, as they were known, were headed by Tex Thornton and included Robert McNamara, who rose to president of Ford at age forty. They implemented systems of statistical analysis in every corner of the company—finance, production, purchasing, sales and marketing, market research, product planning, engineering, and even personnel.

The Whiz Kids became Ford's top management team and turned the company's fortunes around.

The battle for leadership in the industry between Ford and GM continues today. Chrysler was left behind and has been in and out of insolvency and foreign ownership. Chrysler didn't have the size to compete in the mass market against Ford and GM after the war and never had the creativity to compete with the specialty producers in Europe.

The most important development in the post-war years was the rise of the auto industry in Japan and its invasion of foreign markets, particularly in America and Europe. Japan began exporting small, cheap cars to the U.S. in the 1960s. These early models were copied from U.S. designs and engineering. While we were working with Chrysler in the late '70s, a prevalent view was that American buyers wanted big cars and Japan couldn't produce a quality big car. Further, the incremental profit margin on a large car was two to five times larger than that for a small car, so why cannibalize our most profitable sales?

Chrysler was wrong on both counts, though Iacocca became a champion of small cars. Americans would buy small cars because pressure from Congress for fuel efficiency, brought on by the dramatic rise in oil prices and budding environmental concerns would push U.S. consumers to more fuel-efficient automobiles. Japan already produced superb large cars, which I had experienced during my quarterly trips to Japan during the late 1970s, but they also produced quality small cars for the Japanese market.

Just as in so many other industries, post-war Japan entered the auto industry by copying products from other countries, particularly the U.S., and producing them more cheaply. Competitors universally recognized this and maintained their market leadership through better quality. Lower costs, however, allowed Japanese companies to get a foothold in foreign markets, creating an export-driven manufacturing boom in Japan. U.S. competitors in effect ceded the low-cost end of their markets to Japanese exports in autos, industrial machinery, and a number of other manufactured products. U.S. and European companies failed to understand that while Japan's initial products were cheap copies, they diligently studied and modified and improved the quality, performance, and cost of those products. The result was devastating to its competitors as Japan Inc. became an economic force in many world markets.

Even as the early Japanese cars in the U.S. gained popularity and sales, American auto companies actually believed that Japan was little threat. Their denial was stunning and costly. Japanese products rose from a few percent of the U.S. auto market in 1970 to 25 percent in 1990 and one-third by 2000. Their makers began investing in assembly plants in the U.S. in the early 1980s to earn status as locally produced and started designing cars specifically for the U.S. market.

My firm, Booz Allen, was retained by Nissan during the 1980s to find a location for their first new assembly plant in the U.S., with the objective of finding a local labor force that could adopt Japanese manufacturing processes—code for no United Auto Workers (UAW) unions. The Nissan plant in Smyrna, Tennessee, has been considered the most efficient car factory in the world. Thirty-five years after the first U.S.-made Japanese car rolled off an assembly line in Marysville, Ohio, in 1982, the United Auto Workers union has not organized a single Japanese auto plant in this country. Virtually all of the big U.S. auto company plants are represented by the UAW.

In addition to producing quality vehicles, the Japanese had developed extremely efficient processes that involved worker-management cooperation. American unions were a major obstacle to that cooperation. The exclamation point came in 1989, when Toyota undertook a project to develop a luxury car for the U.S. that would be superior to Cadillac and Lincoln in quality, performance, and comfort and could be priced well below imported luxury cars.

The result was the Lexus, which Ford and GM have never been able to match. Finally, in 2008, Toyota became the largest auto producer in the world. During the 1980s and 1990s, I was a member of the

U.S.-Japan Business Council, which included several top executives in the Japanese auto industry. Japan's ambitions were clear. Japan's rise in the U.S. and other foreign markets was well known, but America was still blindsided. Consequently, America lost its undisputed dominance in one of the most important industries in the world economy.

The havoc wrought by this denial of facts and events should be branded on the brain of everyone involved in competitive business. In the global economy, competition can come from anywhere, technology can disrupt any business, and customers will follow their own best interests. The auto industry is a great example, but not a unique one.

In business you need to pay attention to customers and competitors. The company that understands them best is likely to win.

MY INVOLVEMENT IN THE INDUSTRY

By the time I arrived in 1963, Ford was thriving and most of the Whiz Kids had moved on to lead other companies and institutions. Tex Thornton founded Litton Industries, one of the early successful conglomerates, while Bob McNamara had left as president of Ford in 1960 to become Secretary of Defense in the Kennedy Administration and later headed the World Bank. I got to know McNamara years later on the board of the Brookings Institution. Arjay Miller left as president of Ford in 1968 to become dean of the business school at Stanford. One of those remaining was Ed Lundy, Ford's chief financial officer. Lundy had created a financial control system that was instrumental in Ford's success and became the model for many other manufacturing companies.

Lundy's most important contribution, however, was his commitment to hiring and developing the best talent possible. Other companies, such as General Electric, followed his example. Lundy and Ford were early in that game and extraordinarily successful at it. Lundy hired principally from top business schools and always those at the top of their class. Training was instant immersion into Ford's financial control system—eighty-hour weeks were common. No revenue, costs, or investments escaped scrutiny.

Lundy's finance-trained professionals moved into executive positions throughout Ford, throughout GM and Chrysler, and throughout the nation and abroad. Ford became the target of manufacturing companies across the world seeking top corporate finance talent. It was essentially an academy for future CFOs and CEOs.

I was thrilled at the possibility of taking a job under Lundy at Ford. My final interview was with Lundy in his office at Ford World Headquarters at One American Road in Dearborn, Michigan, locally called the Glass House. The finance staff populated the eighth and eleventh floors. Henry Ford II, who was chairman and CEO, and his top management were on the twelfth floor—the inner sanctum.

The environment within the finance staff was invigorating—really smart people, very demanding, and competitive. They thought they were the best unit in the company. I made great friends who came from all over the country. Some bosses were supportive; others would step on your neck to get recognized by their superiors. This was good instruction on how I should operate when it came my turn to be boss. One of my first assignments was to analyze anything Lundy did not include in his formal financial presentation to the board.

In other words, my responsibility was to explain the line item "Other" on the income statement in the unlikely event a board member asked. Lundy wanted to make sure he had an answer for anything, and Other was anything. Not surprisingly, Other was also a huge pile of money with big variances versus budget aggregately offsetting one another. Individual items could be very large. As a result, I had to comb through all the financial statements of the business units to understand variances from budget and the prior year for every item of cost and revenue. I was always prepared, but nobody ever asked about it on my watch. In retrospect it was excellent training, but not very satisfying.

Every experience has value, even if it isn't obvious at the time. For the rest of my career, analyzing operating financials was an important strength.

The most interesting projects were evaluations of investments in new products. For example, a small team of three or four of us evaluated the proposed new 1966 Lincoln Mark car line. The product concept was to build a more luxurious and higher-performance Lincoln off the body shell of the regular Ford car, give it a special name, and hike the price. This was smart and very profitable if it could be pulled off.

Our evaluation was well-prescribed and thorough—a breakdown of investment costs, details on every part and associated labor, marketing and distribution costs, overhead, planned volumes for each model and body style, incremental profit per car, and total profits (including overhead) at planned volumes. We compared the Mark with competing products and assessed the likelihood of meeting their market projections. We had freedom to imagine everything from Mustang-level market success to an Edsel-level disaster . . . and to ask endless questions of the proposers at the Lincoln-Mercury Division. We gave a strong endorsement. The Mark series was approved and became Lincoln's flagship model. It celebrated its fiftieth anniversary a few years ago. There have been more than a dozen iterations.

I mention the details to emphasize the thoroughness and care demanded of us. The process was intense, and many proposals didn't make it through. Divisions making the proposals spent tons of time and talent preparing them. We on the finance staff were the ultimate gatekeepers. A tougher gauntlet I have never seen before or since.

Disciplined, rigorous, fact-based analysis is important for all companies and individuals but is far easier said than done. Start learning to analyze things early in life. It is a skill you must have for success in business.

My time at Ford gave me excellent insight on how auto companies work and on the auto industry in general. As I indicated, the industry has been a great innovator of management processes and techniques—e.g., market-driven product design, financial controls, organization, manufacturing processes, technology integration, and more. Over the next thirty-five years, I would have several direct experiences with auto companies and the opportunity to watch the industry evolve from dominance by three U.S. auto giants into a competitive global industry. I would deal with major changes in technology, products and performance, distribution, manufacturing, and government involvement in a wide range of industries.

BRITISH LEYLAND

My first major project in the auto industry after leaving Ford and joining Booz Allen was with British Leyland in London in the mid-1970s. The new CEO, Sir Michael Edwardes, faced serious problems that were not unlike what a number of other British manufacturing companies were experiencing. U.K. tax rates were extremely high, making capital accumulation to fund investments difficult. The U.K. unions, backed by the Labour government, were at their virulent worst in the mid-1970s. Demands were always higher than companies could afford, and strikes were common, bitter, and long.

Similar to the U.S. experience, the British auto industry began in the early twentieth century with a number of entrepreneurs who built, acquired, and merged with competitors in waves of consolidation. British Leyland Motor Company (BLMC) was the product of the merger of the two largest independent U.K. auto companies, British Motors and Leyland Motors, in 1968. It owned many of the premier British brands—Jaguar, Morris, Austin, MG, Triumph, Leyland, Rover, Mini, Wolseley, Riley, and Daimler. In fact, BLMC had eleven brands and twenty-two models, compared with one or two brands and three to five models for each of its six major European competitors. The merger created the sixth-largest auto company in the world and a set of totally unrealistic expectations. In the following seven years BLMC lost volume and market share, while maintaining the autonomy of most of its product lines. It did not consolidate manufacturing or operations. BLMC appeared headed for failure, prompting the Labour government to take over the company in 1975. Oversight of BLMC was given to a National Enterprise Board (NEB).

Michael Edwardes was brought in by the NEB to do the impossible: turn BLMC into a profitable, growing, world-class competitor in the global automotive industry, based in the U.K. He faced five daunting problems: falling volumes and market shares for almost all product lines; overcapacity across the board; pervasive quality/reliability problems; aging products and power trains in most models; and hostile unions. In addition, there wasn't adequate capital to keep BLMC's wide range of products competitive against better-funded and more-focused U.S., German, and Japanese competitors, and their costs were well above the competition. British Leyland was a mess.

Our task was to determine the viability of their largest manufacturing plants and act as a counselor to Edwardes as he sorted through strategic options. During one of our sessions, Edwardes was dejected at the state of the company. I reminded him that he had some of the most loyal customers in the world. Puzzled, he asked what I meant. My reply: "With all of its product and reliability problems, there are a still a substantial number of Jaguar owners who continue to buy Jaguar. That's loyalty!" For those unfamiliar with Jaguar's history, the car was world famous for beautiful design . . . and for breakdowns—often in the middle of the road—where owners simply abandoned their cars and flagged a taxi.

We jointly concluded with Edwardes that British Leyland could not compete effectively in its current form. Its owner, the U.K. government, wanted BLMC to continue as the country's flagship competitor in the auto industry and to keep manufacturing and ownership in the U.K.

There were three strategic imperatives for BLMC to survive as an independent company: radically rationalize and upgrade the product lines and manufacturing facilities; substantially reduce costs and balance production with realistic sales forecasts; and gain the cooperation of the unions for these radical reforms . . . and do it all with limited infusion of capital from the government.

The correct answer was for the government to allow BLMC to break up the company and sell or close many of its car lines. Few of the product lines were profitable or had the volume to warrant the investment to make them competitive. Short-term cost reductions wouldn't solve their strategic problems. And the unions showed no sign of being cooperative. To his credit, Edwardes won union support, built a stronger management team, and took a mighty whack at the cost structure.

Over the following several years, Edwardes and his successors oversaw the breakup of British Leyland. Some businesses were sold, others shuttered. Many of the product lines have survived and even thrived, though under different owners. Leyland trucks are owned by PACCAR of the U.S. Land Rover; and Range Rover went to BMW, then to Ford, and finally to Tata Industries of India, and remains best in class. Jaguar went to Ford and then Tata. Mini is flourishing under BMW ownership. MG was picked up from liquidation by China's SAIC, which now produces a robust line of MG cars.

The auto industry in the U.K. has had a serious resurgence, though not under U.K. ownership. Local auto production remains at 1.5 million vehicles per year (the same as in the late 1970s) despite the loss of British

Leyland, thanks to Toyota and Honda—and almost 40 percent of U.K. production comes from brands previously owned by BLMC.

British Leyland suffered the strategic dilemma facing many diversified manufacturing companies: too many independent products fighting for limited investment dollars. British Leyland had the additional disadvantage of operating in a country with uncompetitively high taxes and labor costs.

There is nothing shameful about recognizing strategic disadvantages and selling. In fact, the decision to divest a business is as important to shareholders as acquiring a business.

Fortunately, the consolidation of the auto industry was picking up steam at the time British Leyland was divesting. And Margaret Thatcher, a strong voice for free-market capitalism, became Prime Minister. The market, not the government, offered the best solution for British Leyland. The product lines had long, successful histories and strong brand identities, but they needed to be owned by companies that had a strategic need for them and the resources to fund their development into competitive leaders. Free-market capitalism is by far the most efficient way to achieve that result. In BLMC's case the government intervened twice to "save" the British auto industry—first in engineering the merger between British Motors and Leyland Motors and second by taking over British Leyland when it was about to fail. These interventions worsened the situation and delayed the ultimately right answer for the company, its employees, its shareholders, and the country.

Even if sometimes messy, the free market, not government intervention, offers the best solution to most business problems.

BENDIX AND THE AUTO PARTS INDUSTRY

Beginning in 1979, Chrysler became my main occupation. A year or two later, John Day left Chrysler to become CEO of Bendix Corporation and asked Booz Allen to help him turn that company around. Bendix was one of the largest parts manufacturers/suppliers to the auto industry.

In the early days of the auto industry, the companies that assembled and sold the vehicles also manufactured most of the parts needed for their cars. By the late 1970s, driven by economics, the majority of the components were manufactured by independent parts companies. The resulting supplier industry was large and competitive.

The perspective of the auto assemblers was very different from the suppliers. Product and technology development had once been solely in the hands of the automakers. Parts makers were now doing research and development. Bendix became a leader in several high-tech areas, most notably brake systems.

The auto industry was on the cusp of an explosion of technology. Engines, steering, braking, materials, CAD/CAM (computer aided design and manufacturing), emission controls, mileage improvements, navigation, entertainment systems, electronics, and safety aids such as seat belts, airbags, and impact-absorbing structures were all targets for improvement by the auto and parts makers. We worked together with Day and Bendix for a year, first to improve profitability and then to position Bendix to be a leader in its industry in the future.

While there were extraordinary changes in the auto industry in my lifetime, there will be upheavals as dramatic and sweeping in the decades ahead. As I write this book, a South African–born entrepreneur, Elon Musk, has become a multibillionaire by producing the Tesla electric car, and Google and Uber are testing self-driving cars. The market value of Tesla has surpassed Ford, GM, and Chrysler-Fiat combined!

Imagine when electric cars become the majority of cars on the road, as is likely by 2050. What will that do to the oil industry, or to the service stations that cover our landscape? And what will happen to employment if all cars are self-driven? Drivers (taxis, trucks, etc.) may be the largest source of employment for non-college people today. You need to be prepared for these and many other possibilities we can't even imagine.

As you go through your career, look critically at your own organizations and the evolution of their industries. You and your company should develop the innovations that make obsolete your own products. Be a constructive disrupter in your company. Why let a competitor obsolete you?

A former CEO of General Motors, Rick Waggoner, told me that driverless cars were almost certain to dominate sales within twenty years and will dominate the roads in forty to fifty years. The only reason it will take that long is the prohibitive cost of retrofitting or replacing the 1.2 billion registered vehicles on the road today. There will be other changes driven by technology, environmental regulations, economics, and customer interests—and they could come from anywhere. The auto industry will likely continue to be a major player in the world's economy, but don't count on the current companies in the industry to lead in the future.

Opportunities are always there for the creative and bold.

TRANSFORMATION

Over my lifetime, the auto industry has become a major part of the world economy, and it has transformed our way of life. The automobile revolution ranks with other tectonic changes in the past century—agriculture, energy, medicine and medical devices, telecommunications, jet airplanes, and the internet. The automobile changed the landscape of our country, enabling cities to expand into suburbs and altering our way of life by putting instant transportation at the doorstep of the vast majority of people. I have been fortunate to have been both an observer of the industry's impact on society and a participant in its transition. The auto industry taught me what makes businesses successful as well as some of the important mistakes corporate chiefs and industry leaders can make.

There is a world of valuable knowledge available to those who pay attention to why some companies succeed and others fail, about why some industries grow profitably and others are blindsided by developments. All experiences have value to those who are aware and perceptive.

Chapter Four

WHAT IS MANAGEMENT CONSULTING?

Booz Allen was my career for thirty-five years and nine months—an almost unprecedented length of time with one firm these days. The simple reason: I found a profession I loved. It challenged me continually, and it brought out the best in me. Each assignment—indeed, each day—was approached with excitement and determination. In other words, I committed myself and delivered. You may be asking "Why?"

At Booz Allen there weren't many rungs on the ladder—only three steps to partner and one more to senior partner. Everyone worked with clients, from the CEO down to the newest consultant. We knew our clients personally, their problems were our problems, and their success was our success.

In most businesses there are so many strata that the company's vision and strategy are lost as you get farther from the corner office. In a professional service firm everyone understands what your business is and how it can succeed, and everyone participates in its core activities. Everyone, including its leaders, is actively involved with clients. That should be the same for all professional firms—law, accounting, investing, advertising, medicine, engineering, banking, education, as well as management consulting.

At Booz Allen there was a true sense of partnership. Cooperation and mutual support were shared values. From day one, all professionals were on a first-name basis, although it was awkward for me to call Mr. Allen "Jim," but we all did. Booz Allen was a meritocracy with service to clients as the most important yardstick and ability to deal effectively with colleagues a close second.

Management consulting has its own set of skills that are necessary in order to work with clients who know their company better than the consultant does: Objectivity, Listening, Curiosity, Understanding, Analytics, Discipline, Communications, and Focus. And there was one characteristic common to all consultants who made it past a year or two: Intelligence. This made the working environment exciting and invigorating.

A word on *listening*. Good listening doesn't mean agreeing. It means understanding. You learn far more by listening than by talking.

During my work life, I rarely averaged more than 20 percent of my time in the office. When you are a consultant, you are with your clients. Even when the client was in town, our work occurred at the client's site. Consultants were often assigned to a client for months at a time. When an assignment was completed, we were on to the next one, often in a different city, a different industry, or even a different country. Partners had multiple clients at the same time and were able to manage more nights at home than the consultant with one client in Dubuque. My experience as a road warrior was awful in my first year, then somewhat better in the next several years until we moved to Paris, where I had responsibility for our international practice and was away a ridiculous amount of time. Those were tough years on the family and on me.

MY FIRST ASSIGNMENT

Sam Beacham, who was responsible for staffing client engagements, called with my first assignment. Sam matched the consultants, each with different skills, experience, interests, and development needs, with incoming engagements. I had just finished "Charm School," an intense two weeks of training in the consulting profession. I liked what I heard. There were similarities with Ford, such as analytical rigor, good facility with numbers, project focused—but important differences, including far less structure and supervision, more variety, and exposure to top management.

The client was Dresser Industries, a maker of industrial equipment, and the assignment was a confidential assessment of Link-Belt as an acquisition candidate. Link-Belt produced earth-moving equipment, which was a logical extension of Dresser's product line. I discuss it here to give you an idea of what boot consultants can expect, and because it was the beginning of my new career. We had about ten weeks and couldn't contact Link-Belt or let anyone know what we were doing. Hmmmmm. Jack Page was the handling officer and reported to Ed Morse, a senior partner in a corner office in Booz Allen headquarters in the Field Building at 135 South LaSalle Street, Suite 1700, Chicago.

I, on the other hand, had no office. Each morning the consultants came in as supplicants to the all-powerful receptionist, whose most important job (from the consultants' point of view) was assigning consultants to offices not occupied by their owners that day. Once those openings were exhausted, the remaining consultants went to the bullpen, a large room with tables where it was impossible to concentrate. There was a strong incentive to work in the client's offices and to be promoted so you were assigned a permanent desk of your own. I knew that I had to get on the right side of Ms. All-Powerful. Complaining when given a bad office or the bullpen was not the best approach. A charm offensive was in order, as was arriving early. Whatever I did, it worked. The few times I was sentenced to the bullpen, she apologized.

Typically there was a project manager between the partner and the consultant, but in this case there wasn't, so I worked directly with Page. He had great patience with the newbie as I stopped by his office for the eighth time in a day. We developed a work plan that began with the goal: what we had to deliver to the client. Step two: determine the questions that had to be answered and identify, obtain, and verify the information needed to solve the problem. Remember, this was long before Google. Third, the toughest part, was analyzing the information and developing options for the client. Finally, we had to determine our recommendations for the client with a rationale that would compel them to act.

Armed with the work plan, I got busy on the first assignment in my new career. We developed the list of issues we needed to address and the information we needed for each. We then selected a number of suppliers, customers, competitors, and industry experts to contact. I read all about the heavy construction industry and the firms in it, including everything I could get my eyes on about Link-Belt and Dresser Industries. My starting point was zero, although I had seen a front-end loader. During the next several weeks I buried myself in the industry—the economics, the performance, the factors for success, profit drivers, strengths/weaknesses, and reputations of the key competitors, particularly of Link-Belt. We looked for the fits between Dresser and Link-Belt—product lines, manufacturing, customer industries, supply lines, distribution, engineering—and took a crack at synergies from a merger. Most of my interviews were by telephone. It was amazing how open people were when I told them I was with Booz Allen. It was almost like they were trying to get the prize for giving the most information. Every few days I checked in with Page. He seemed to think we were making good progress.

A couple of weeks before D-day with the client, Page told me to put together a report. He gave me some guidance about what Booz Allen reports looked like and what it should say and concluded that he didn't want a draft. He wanted the final report ready to be delivered to the client. I repeated what he said to make sure I understood what I thought to be an insane request. I had never written a report, and he wanted me to have it client-ready? Yes, he said, client-ready. Off I went on my mission. I put together the report I would want as a client from a consultant, checked and rechecked my data, and made a few calls to verify things that seemed in conflict with other data.

The next step learned from Charm School was to submit it to the editor, who had been with the firm since the beginning of time and who trashed every report she saw to make it suitable for the client. She proceeded to rip my work apart, catching every instance of twisted syntax and inconsistency.

Next was printing. We printed our client reports and put them between hard covers anchored with screws and posts. Seems quaint in view of current technology, but they were so elegant, so serious, so professional . . . so inefficient. On the appointed day I put five copies of the final report on Page's desk. He all but fainted. In addition to his review, he had to review the report with Ed Morse. Morse laughed uncontrollably. Happily, the only change made from my "final" version was a page of conclusions that Morse added at the end.

The following week we had our meeting with Dresser's CEO and his team. Morse and Page asked me to join. Page took them through the report but tossed questions to me. The client group was riveted. We demonstrated the excellent fit in customers, engineering, manufacturing, and product lines. Skills were complementary. Synergy was substantial. Link-Belt's reputation was excellent and market position was strong. The meeting ended well, and we were thanked for doing a good job. I was walking on air.

A few months later, Dresser made an offer to acquire Link-Belt, which set off a bidding war between Dresser and FMC Corp. FMC eventually won and acquired Link-Belt a few months later. I have always thought that Dresser missed a good one.

On your first project for any new job, give it your all. Dive in. Don't waste a lot of time wandering around learning the ropes.

I had five client engagements in my first year with four different partners. Learning the ropes meant working with as many partners as possible, and with different client problems.

In the 1960s, management consulting was in its early stages. Booz Allen was reported by *BusinessWeek* to be the largest U.S. management consulting firm with $36 million in revenues. Management consultants had begun to morph from smart generalists to experienced experts. I had joined the profession as a problem solver who would jump into any situation. It was clear that consulting was moving toward specialists deep in an industry or possessing a functional skill like manufacturing technology, information systems, product development, or strategy.

In fact, the change came more quickly than most anticipated. Over the next decade, new entrants like Boston Consulting Group and Bain changed strategy consulting. Accounting firms such as Arthur Andersen and Touche Ross bet heavily on information systems, followed by the other major accounting firms. Many other specialized firms emerged. The market for management consulting was exploding, and Booz Allen and McKinsey continued to grow rapidly despite the new entrants.

We were also discovering that we did some things the new specialty firms couldn't—particularly counseling with a client's CEO and board. Despite the scramble to adopt or acquire new technologies, we had to be careful not to lose our advantage of entrée to the C-suite. I understood and supported the need for special expertise but also knew that my personal DNA required diversity. I would always be moving on to new things. In addition, I have always thought that the best CEOs and political leaders were people who had a broad range of experiences.

It's the same argument that promotes liberal arts as the best preparation for leadership. Leaders are continually confronted with problems that have no labels or precedents but require an ability to see and understand the important elements of highly complex situations. I will never be a successful research scientist—not enough patience. But I believed I was preparing myself for leadership . . . of something. For the time being, I had to do my best at anything I undertook.

BURTON-DIXIE MATTRESS COMPANY

Joe Kubert had the reputation of being the toughest, most demanding partner in the Chicago office. Clients respected him because he pulled no punches and solved their problems. Consultants at my level feared him. In my casual encounters, he seemed very smart, direct, and reasonable. I asked Sam Beacham to put me on one of his engagements. Kubert summoned me to his office for an interview. "Why do you want to work with me?" came before "Hello." I responded politely, "Because I heard you were a great consultant and I could learn from you." "What makes you think you're good enough?" Another softball question. You get the idea. He loved his tough-guy image and reinforced it constantly. It appeared to me that Kubert felt this was the best way to get consultants to work harder and smarter. This leadership style was prevalent in Ford's manufacturing divisions. You had to be the toughest, baddest hombre in the pack to get to the top of the mountain, and a few kills along the way were a plus. Bill Sick had shown me how to tame the hombres—perform.

Sam reported back to me that Kubert had a project for me—the Burton-Dixie Mattress Company. It's included here as a good example of the breadth of problems and situations we dealt with and the hoops necessary to develop into a good consultant. Also, it was amusing.

Burton-Dixie was still a recognized name in the mattress business in the 1960s. Decades earlier it had been a leader, but tough times had fallen on the company. Our task: Give the owners/management an objective assessment of its prospects. Kubert was a good friend of the CEO and hoped we could help him save the company. Our budget was tight so we had a small team—of one. The project was totally different from my other engagements. The other clients were large, healthy, growing companies. Burton-Dixie was small and on the ropes in a competitive segment of the retail industry.

Since this was my fourth or fifth client engagement, I knew the drill. I reviewed my work plan with Kubert, who made some helpful suggestions that could have been mistaken for criticisms. I immediately dove into fact-gathering, learning as much as possible about Burton-Dixie and the mattress business.

In its heyday, Burton-Dixie had eight plants across the country and its Slumberon brand had been a market leader, a proud and successful Chicago-based company. Now it competed in the commodity segment of its market with razor-thin margins. Its market share was a fraction of the market leaders'; product design and quality were only suitable for the low-end market. Think Motel 6. Its mattress business was losing money. Sales had been declining for several years, and they were down to one mattress plant in the Bedford-Stuyvesant section of Brooklyn. It looked hopeless. Financials matched its strategic position—negative cash flow for the mattress business and a modest positive cash flow for the company because of its auto seat business. Overheads had already been reduced substantially, so no solution there.

I visited the plant to see if there was anything that could be done with it to help the financial picture—e.g., cost reduction, productivity improvement, maybe contract manufacturer for retailers. I got my first signal when a cab driver refused to take me from my New York hotel to the plant. I flagged another cab and got in before telling him where I was going. He developed engine trouble a block later after hearing our destination. The third try worked. I told the driver I didn't have the address but knew the directions.

The plant was surrounded by a barbed wire fence and other defenses that were more appropriate for an embassy in a war-torn country than for a U.S. manufacturing plant. I met the plant manager, a woman around fifty who looked the part of a prison warden. She gave me "the tour." Think of a factory in England in the late eighteenth century—no automation, lots of workers cutting, sewing, packing, carrying, stacking. Lots of motion, but no clear workflow. The few machines were early industrial-revolution vintage. A team kept them running with oil cans and hammers. Everyone looked tough, apparently for good reason. She told me that her most serious problem was worker safety traveling between home and the factory. Once inside the plant, the workers were safe—their few cars parked outside, not so much. Kubert seemed unfazed by my report. He made a comment that I remember to this day: "Just shows you that a business can keep operating long after it's dead."

There was one more thing to explore. Burton-Dixie about a decade earlier had begun supplying auto manufacturers with car seats made from sisal. They would stuff sisal, which was like hay, into a metal frame and cover it with cloth, plastic, or leather, quite similar to making a mattress in George Washington's time. The auto seat business had been keeping the company afloat. Margins were good, with enough volume to more than cover the losses in the mattress business. We visited the major auto companies to discuss auto seats and Burton-Dixie and received an ominous message. The U.S. auto industry was switching their seats to molded foam over five years. They were one year into the process, and the customer reaction was so positive that they were considering accelerating the conversion. Costs were lower, quality control was much better, and customers preferred foam seats. That was it for Burton-Dixie. How could they not have known?

Kubert asked me to present our findings orally (no written report) to the CEO. I outlined the next steps: close the mattress business and sell what assets they could; continue to serve the auto companies until cash flow turned negative; and either seek new businesses to buy or close the doors. Kubert gave a summary at the end, which was, in effect, the eulogy for Burton-Dixie Mattress Co.

Joe and I worked together a number of times and became good friends. He died as he lived, going flank speed. He and his son were mountain climbing, and Joe suffered a fatal heart attack. I was very sad, because Joe Kubert was a real professional who taught me a lot.

Sometimes the toughest bosses give you the most valuable experiences. Judge bosses on their value to your common mission and to your development rather than on their demeanor.

ELECTION TO PARTNER

At the end of each assignment, all members of the team were given formal written reviews. Mine had been consistently positive on consulting skills and problem solving. There was concern that I was too demanding of other staff members and too impatient to move up. They were probably right on both counts, but I was behind after four years in the military, and my consultant peers were two to four years younger. Nevertheless, I was elected partner in April 1969.

Life did change as a partner. Partners were judged both by the quality of their work and by the clients they brought to the firm. I had to learn to develop business. There are three sources of business in consulting: expanding work with current clients; selling engagements to clients who call us; and attracting new clients. I had been doing the first through developing professional relations with clients and understanding their companies beyond the current projects. Now was the time to demonstrate my ability to convert inquiries into clients. The third, attracting new clients, would come later. In my first few years as a partner, I was given a number of inquiries from small and medium-sized companies. A cynical observer would say they were the leftovers. For me, they were perfect learning opportunities.

Typical was the Jasper Saw Company of Jasper, Indiana. The owner was turning over management of the company to his thirty-year-old son, but the handoff was not going well. He had been told by a friend that he should contact Booz Allen. A meeting was set with the owner. "Can you help me save my company and my son?" was his only question. A year of working shoulder to shoulder with the new CEO and watching the company turn upward as he grew in confidence was truly rewarding.

In another case, a real estate developer was establishing a new integrated real estate firm from development through property management and wanted help in setting up his organization, developing a strategy, and launching his company. Neither of us had experience in starting a new company, but together we made it happen successfully. In another case, a Caterpillar engine franchisee wanted a strategy for expanding his business. In the process, I helped the client define what options he had for expanding his business and proposed a plan of action. Once we won an engagement, I was in my comfort zone.

As you learn your profession, understand its requirements and use every opportunity to build the necessary skills.

In addition to the inquiries from small companies, I worked with several larger firms, such as Allis-Chalmers in Milwaukee, for which we did several studies on costs and productivity and a search for a new CFO. At the Tribune Company in Chicago, we analyzed the profitability and prospects of their newsprint paper manufacturing facility in Canada to determine whether they should stay in that business. AT&T asked how they should integrate marketing into their business. Imagine that! Bandag, the country's largest truck tire retreader, sought to diversify.

I thrived on the diversity, from small, family-owned companies to big conglomerates, from start-ups to established leaders. And in every case, we reported directly to the CEO and worked with top management. In almost every case, the client acted on our recommendations.

ALLIS-CHALMERS

Allis-Chalmers was an example of a troubled old-line manufacturer that sought our advice. I relate this example because the real problem was different from what the CEO perceived, and ultimately it was a good example of how the capitalist system works. David Scott, chief executive officer of the manufacturer of farm equipment and industrial machinery, called Bill Monroe, a longtime partner in our Chicago office, to help with its turnaround. Scott came from Colt Industries and before that General Electric. He had been in most of the executive chairs but was particularly deep in heavy-equipment manufacturing. Bill asked me, a newly minted partner, to join him.

Scott's mandate was to halt the company's slide in sales and profits. He had already kicked off a major restructuring program, but it wasn't going smoothly. In Scott's view, the problem was in manufacturing, particularly in its farm equipment business. More than half of the company's reported earnings were attributed to financing dealer and customer purchases of its equipment. About half of Allis-Chalmers' sales came from its unprofitable farm equipment business. It did make money on parts. The only manufacturing business in the company producing good profits made electric power generators, and was also the only market share leader in its industry.

We fielded three teams and dug into each business. There were considerable opportunities for profit improvement across the board. There were two conclusions, however, that caused serious debate. First, the finance company, which was considered the "golden goose" and had untouchable status in the company, was completely dependent on sales of the manufacturing businesses, particularly farm equipment. A sale or major downsizing of farm equipment would cut the finance company's profits significantly. A big chunk of financing was to dealers for their inventory. Equipment sent to dealers was counted as a sale on Allis-Chalmers's books—presto, a sale and profit were reported, along with the interest on the loan to the dealer and customer. A serious downturn could crush the company financially.

Our second conclusion was strategic. With the exception of the generator business, Allis-Chalmers was a second-tier player in highly competitive, capital-intensive businesses. These businesses were subscale in manufacturing and had market shares that were a fraction of those of the industry leaders—most below 10 percent. These translated into cost-and-market competitive disadvantages, which are very difficult to remedy without major investment. In addition, Allis-Chalmers competed in about twenty different businesses, each of which had market leaders that were multiples of its size, but the company still required investments in each to be competitive. Allis-Chalmers had to spread its investment dollars while its competitors focused theirs. It had grown through five decades by acquiring small companies in a wide range of industrial equipment. In effect, Allis-Chalmers, a machinery conglomerate, was fighting against focused giants—like Deere and Caterpillar in the U.S. and Komatsu, Fiat, and Siemens internationally—with BB guns versus howitzers.

Thus the debate: Take action now to improve profitability, or attack the strategic issue through rebuilding the company around those businesses that could become leaders either through acquisitions, joint ventures, or major investments. Under pressure from shareholders and his board, the CEO chose the short-term improvement course. As expected, profits rose, with cuts in expenses resulting in a few years of good profits and rising stock price. Nevertheless, the next recession pushed Allis-Chalmers to the brink of bankruptcy and substantially weakened its ability to come back. Over the next decade, the CEO explored partners for several of its businesses, forming Fiat-Allis in construction equipment and the Siemens-Allis alliance in the electrical controls market, both of which were subsequently taken over by their stronger partners.

Fast-forward to after I had returned to Chicago from my eight-year tour overseas, Wendell Bueche, the new CEO of Allis-Chalmers, called. The story was the same as on my initial work a decade before. Bueche, an avid Notre Dame grad five years ahead of me, took over from Scott after the company lost $200 million on sales of $1.6 billion. Bueche, formerly the CFO, understood the strategic weaknesses. We hit it off perfectly and attacked the strategic issues. We worked together to improve several businesses, prepare for sale or alliances, and ultimately liquidate what was left of Allis-Chalmers. The good businesses found new homes and continued to be successful. The weaker businesses were absorbed by larger competitors or shut down.

Allis-Chalmers was a good example of how capitalism works. If a company cannot survive in the market, its good parts are sold to stronger companies, which meld their operations to reduce costs and improve products. The weak parts are shut down. Managers are redeployed elsewhere in the economy. These transitions can be painful to shareholders, bankers, and displaced employees, but the process assures that the strongest companies survive and the weakest depart the scene, which is the right answer to strengthen and grow the economy. The market decides who stays and who goes, not the government.

Coming up with the right answer is only half the game. Getting the company to act and execute successfully is equally important. And a good consultant must do both.

Outside consultants have influence but no power to execute. Put yourself in a position to have strong influence. A close relationship based on mutual trust and respect with the decision maker (i.e., the CEO) is key.

As a consequence of my work with several companies in distress or undergoing difficult transitions, I learned important fundamentals about turning companies around. These experiences led me to focus on companies facing major transitions—companies like COSIPA (a Brazilian steel company), British Leyland, Chrysler, United Airlines, Amoco, and Monsanto as a consultant, Chiquita and the Sun-Times Media Group as CEO, and HSBC USA and Allegheny Energy as a board member.

Focus on and build expertise in areas in which you are strong and that you enjoy. Build a reputation.

WHAT NEXT?

In 1971, five years after joining the firm, I was at a crossroads. Unquestionably, I had learned more and enjoyed the work more than I ever could have imagined. But my learning curve was about to plateau. Despite the variety of engagements, doing the same thing for the next twenty-five—or even five—years didn't feel right. Should I continue in consulting or move on to something else? If I continued, what should I do within Booz Allen? I had no interest in joining another consulting firm. I was already with the best, in my view. While there was an itch to look outside the firm, my trajectory internally was excellent, and I truly enjoyed what I was doing. The work was challenging, fun, and impactful to client organizations. Becoming a member of the top management team in a reasonable period of time looked possible. Consequently, I decided to delay looking outside if there was a move into the firm's management, which meant taking over an office. I counseled with everyone, including Jim Allen, about what would be best for me and for the firm. The consensus was that I was ready to run an office but would have to move.

My first five years taught me how to be an effective consultant. Along the way, I had the satisfaction of helping several organizations perform better. The experience confirmed my belief that consulting was and could continue to be a rewarding career.

Continually look to the future in your career. When it's time to move up or move on, *move*.

BUSINESS: THE ULTIMATE TEAM SPORT

One of the most important lessons I learned in those first five years working with twenty or so client corporations was the striking similarities between team sports and business. In sports, the consistent winners have the best players in each position, the best training, the most discipline, the best teamwork, the best coach and team leadership, the best understanding of competitors, the best strategy and game plans, and they are the most motivated, particularly in the clutch. That formula for winning is exactly the same in business.

Both sports and business are competitive games, pitting teams in the same fields and using scoreboards to measure success. Team sports require teamwork among the players, putting the interest of the team ahead of self-interest. Both sports and business have superstars. The most successful understand that a team win is more important than personal stats. It is not surprising that many successful business leaders were good in sports.

Personally I loved competitive sports and found the same competitive exhilaration in business. The stakes and the size of the teams, however, were orders of magnitude greater in business.

Chapter Five

SIN, OUI, SI, JA, DA, HAI, AREH, YES!

The decision on my next step with Booz Allen was important for me professionally. The choice between Cleveland and São Paulo, Brazil, the two offices open to me, was easy. The greater independence and international experience of Brazil were appealing. The following eight years in Brazil and France with Booz Allen were outstanding, both professionally and for the family. My time abroad presented a fresh set of challenges and offered experiences that would guide me throughout the rest of my career. The opportunity to live and work in different cultures, political systems, and economic philosophies and conditions was extraordinary both for me and my family. The education in life and the world were unmatched for our three almost perfect children.

Understanding that the world is a complex network of different cultures gave me an advantage in building relationships socially and in business—not just in Brazil and France but anywhere, because I grew to understand that there are differences and knew how to deal with them. I learned particularly not to be judgmental. I could (and did) do business anywhere without stumbling on cultural barriers.

(A Big Lesson) Don't stay in your lane. If you have the opportunity to live abroad, consider it very seriously. It can enrich your life and your outlook. You won't fall behind the folks at headquarters—you'll jump over them. And it can be a game changer for your family.

Working in more than twenty countries, I experienced the good and the bad in economic systems—free-market capitalism, central planning in military dictatorships, various forms of economic socialism. Just as this is not a history book, it is not a treatise on economic systems. However, I will offer observations about how various systems help or impede the success of companies and impact their countries. Those wishing a deeper understanding of economic systems—and I would encourage you to learn—should research the copious literature on them.

My missions in Brazil and France were different. In Brazil, my task was to build a business in that country, which was similar to my experience in Chicago, although as the leader of a new team rather than as a member of a well-developed team. In France, my mission was to establish Booz Allen as the leading management consulting firm outside North America.

BRAZIL

Throughout the past century, Brazil has been governed by a succession of military and civilian governments, starting with the military coup that replaced the emperor and established a republic in 1889. There were three more military coups in the ensuing eighty years. When we arrived in January 1972, Brazil had been governed by a military dictatorship since 1964. The country's motto on its flag, *Ordem e Progresso*—Order and Progress—explains the frequent interventions of the military when more order was required. General Emílio Médici and General Ernesto Geisel were presidents while we were in Brazil.

Brazil was a large, diverse country with great wealth and great poverty. About 25 percent of its 150 million population lived in a handful of urban centers. São Paulo was the largest. Poverty was widespread and grinding. The graphic example of the life of the poor was the favelas (slums) in Rio—a large camp-like settlement of thousands living in primitive conditions. A movie about the favelas in Rio, *City of God,* showed the world what serious poverty looked and felt like. The social programs to help the poor were minimal, and crime was rampant. The political opposition was violent—several kidnappings of highly placed politicians and foreign businessmen for ransom. (It happened to one of our neighbors.)

The government's response was aggressive—many opposition agitators were killed by the police. A "Wanted" poster hung in public places with the pictures of forty to fifty mostly men. They didn't change the poster but merely put a thick black "X" across the pictures of people who were eliminated. High-profile foreigners had bodyguards and took measures to protect their families. Another neighbor, the president of Ford of Brazil, had several armed bodyguards and traveled in two identical vehicles.

On the other hand, the Brazilians are a joyful people. Those we came in contact with socially, in business, and in everyday activities were delightful. Foreigners were welcomed. Life was tough for people at the bottom of the economic ladder, but they worked hard and seemed happy—enjoying kids, dogs, samba, and *futebol.* Brazilians *love futebol* (soccer) and their success in the World Cup (its five wins are still top in the world) is a gigantic source of national pride. When we arrived in 1972, Brazil held the Cup from their 1970 win in Mexico with Pelé, who was retiring after winning three of the previous four World Cups. I had asked a Brazilian executive, "Who will be the next Pelé?" Response: "That's like asking who will be the next Jesus Christ." I remember asking a shoeshine boy, "Who is the president of Brazil?" He didn't know. Then I asked who was on Brazil's national soccer team. He was encyclopedic about every player, even those on the bench.

The Brazilian "Economic Miracle" was in full swing when we arrived. The average annual GDP growth rate for 1967–1979 was 9 percent. Inflation had been a serious problem for Brazil since the Second World War. The inflation rate while we were in Brazil was moderate in historical terms—15 to 20 percent. It shot to 110 percent by 1980. I keep an old 100,000 cruzeiro note in my study. In 1972 its value in U.S. dollars was $20,000; in 2000 its value was a fraction of one cent. A stern reminder of the impact of inflation. The timing of collections and payments was crucial as prices changed often, even daily—never keep extra cash in the drawer. The joke among Brazilians was, "You know inflation is bad when the bus fare taking you home is higher than the fare that morning going to work."

About half of the economy had been owned or controlled by the government since the military coup at the end of the Second World War—oil, steel, mining, telecommunications, electricity, railroads, airlines, and most large commercial and development banks were nationalized. There was no competition in these sectors except for banking. State-owned enterprises (SOEs) were created by the government to manage these sectors. The government appointed boards and executives to run the SOEs. SOEs accounted for about 40 percent of Brazil's economy. Booz Allen's clients were steel SOEs.

State-owned enterprises are common in developing countries. The rationale—most of the industries chosen are key to building a modern industrial-based economy, and there were few groups in the private sector with adequate capital. Establishing SOEs in key sectors was a means of kick-starting industrialization of the economy. In addition, the World Bank funded many SOEs in the developing world to get those economies on their feet. The big disadvantage was that SOEs are virtually all less efficient and less competitive than privately run companies in the same industries. SOEs were controlled by the government and had political missions such as employment, housing, healthcare, and education of workers. Managers were chosen by politicians who put loyalty and political aims ahead of experience and expertise. Most important, the government rather than the market sets prices and production levels and allocates resources, which results in major market inefficiencies. SOEs control local markets through government regulation and monopolies. Competition is simply not allowed. Most SOEs cannot meet international standards to be competitive with foreign-made products without substantial subsidies. Few, if any, SOEs are able to compete in global markets, where competitive quality, costs, and service win. The correct answer, in my view, is to launch a capital-intensive industry through an SOE where necessary, but turn it over to the private sector as soon as it is up and running. Competition is a superb discipline for improving— either you meet competitive standards or you go away.

Foreign firms were major players in Brazil's highly regulated private sector, both through imports and local investment and production— particularly autos, chemicals, pharmaceuticals, industrial machinery, information technology, and consumer products. There were tight regulations governing imports, exports, currency transfers, and a wide range of business transactions. Brazil had a robust industrial economy. The economy, however, was not based on free-market capitalism. The government intervened everywhere, with its finger on the scales to meet its political objectives. Agriculture, mining, and textiles were Brazil's largest indigenous industries, and raw materials and farm products accounted for most of Brazil's exports. Brazil had discovered large oil deposits offshore but had not yet developed them. Historically Brazil's economy was built on agricultural products, particularly coffee. (Ever hear "The Coffee Song [They've Got an Awful Lot of Coffee in Brazil]"?)

Brazil had long been considered to have the potential to become one of the world's great economies. The country was rich in mineral resources and was the fifth largest in arable land behind the U.S., India, Russia, and China. Political instability, a low rate of literacy, and bad policy choices, however, have prevented Brazil from realizing its potential. Brazil was clearly part of the developing world when we arrived.

They were striving to join the developed world of Western Europe, North America, and Japan. Their objective was to develop an industrial base domestically to supplement their agricultural and mining strength. Their industrial base was historically weak and depended heavily on foreign technology and imports.

Post–World War II, Brazil instituted an Industrial Policy to control the economy centrally. Step one: Nationalize basic industries and set up SOEs to run them. Step two: Determine which additional industries should be planned and controlled centrally and put technocrats in charge of running or regulating these industries. Step three: Replace imports with locally manufactured products through an import substitution program. The government set tariffs and regulations to drive out imports in targeted sectors, encouraged foreign firms to manufacture in Brazil, and financed national firms to build facilities to manufacture locally. Brazil was in the middle of implementing these policies when we arrived. Understanding what they were attempting to achieve and how was important for me.

As you enter any new assignment, it is essential to understand the rules of the game and the objectives of your customers/clients.

One of the biggest problems with a centrally controlled economy is that priorities and the allocation of resources are determined by the government rather than the market. Throughout history this has resulted in overcapacity in some areas, shortages in others, and inefficiencies everywhere. That was one of the fundamental flaws of Marxism/communism and various forms of socialism. Brazil's model was a derivative of capitalism with heavy central control—state-controlled capitalism. Brazil did not pursue redistribution of wealth as communism and socialism do, so the profit motive was very much alive. My job was to help companies manage themselves more effectively, not to change their economic model.

The economic situation in Brazil was the best in Latin America in the early 1970s. Productivity was growing, unemployment low, and confidence off the charts. The military government was supportive of economic growth and welcomed foreign firms. Since state-owned companies accounted for 40 percent of the economy, it was in the government's interest for these companies to be well run. The remainder of the economy was modified free-market capitalism. The cruzeiro was not a freely traded currency, so international transactions were controlled by the government. The level of government control was an encumbrance to the flexibility of all companies to chart their own courses, but Brazil was closer to a capitalist economy than most in the developing world.

When we arrived, Booz Allen had two clients, both SOEs in the steel business. The contract with our larger client, COSIPA, the steel company owned and operated by the state of São Paulo, was set to expire in a few months. Our work with our other client, USIMINAS, the state-owned steel company of Minas Gerais, Brazil's fourth-largest state, was in the final stages of winding down. We had about twelve professionals who would be without work very shortly. All but two were steel experts and American expatriates who were expensive to maintain in Brazil. And the client pipeline was empty. Nothing like the gallows to focus one's attention.

My mission was to establish the firm in Brazil by building a broad clientele. My plan was first to build on the clients and staff we had; second to become involved in corporate and government circles to meet potential clients; and third to build and train a staff of local Brazilians and inject a few experienced Americans. The new factor was that we had only a few months to get things moving.

My first priority was to assure that we were serving our current clients well. We met with both CEOs. We had been working with USIMINAS in Belo Horizonte for several years. CEO Amaro Lanari had built USIMINAS into arguably the most successful steel company in South America. Our firm had assisted him is several areas of operations, strategy, and organization. During our presentation of the results of our review, we noted that inventories were very high, particularly in raw materials, maintenance parts, and equipment. Lanari calmly explained that they were a government company and the inventories were his "bank," which allowed him to keep operating if the government cut funds for whatever reason. Our conclusion was that USIMINAS was doing fine and that we should keep close to Lanari and stand ready to help when needed. And I learned a good lesson about state-owned enterprises.

State-owned enterprises are subject to political decisions and pressures, and planning for "rainy days" can take unusual forms.

COSIPA

Our work with COSIPA began a few years earlier as a result of a loan from the World Bank to fund expansion of its steel production. Our firm had been retained to develop the organization and systems to manage the expansion project. It was clear to both the client and our team that continued assistance would be necessary beyond the end of the current contract. I believed we should significantly broaden our mandate.

Our lead professional in Brazil, Doug Purvance, and I conducted a review of the entire company to determine (1) its ability to complete the expansion project successfully, and (2) its readiness to become a successful steel producer—technically up-to-date, efficient, cost-competitive, profitable, with a management team and processes to successfully run the larger company. We found its ability to complete the expansion to be on plan, but its readiness to manage the larger company inadequate.

While COSIPA had good facilities and international technical support, it had lacked management processes—not uncommon for government-owned companies. The company's organization, production planning, budgeting and cost control, management training and development, customer service, and coordination and oversight at all levels needed substantial upgrading. The question was how to convince COSIPA's management of the necessity and the World Bank to fund it. Fortunately, the World Bank had a major stake in COSIPA, its largest loan in Latin America.

Mario Leon was the CEO. Like CEOs of most government-owned enterprises, Leon had a career in government and academia and was appointed to run COSIPA because government leaders trusted him, not because he had experience in the industry or in running large companies. Like most SOEs in Brazil, COSIPA had technical partnerships with international firms. Management experience, however, was limited everywhere.

COSIPA was a blank canvas ready for someone to help them create an effective organization to run their new company with new state-of-the-art facilities. The World Bank often required its loan clients to hire consultants to track projects they were financing, such as our ongoing work with COSIPA. My conclusion was that "tracking the project" would provide the World Bank with a warning of failure but wouldn't prevent it. Further, having great state-of-the-art facilities was important but didn't guarantee success without effective management.

Purvance and I met with the World Bank representative in Brazil to lay out our ideas about how we would assist COSIPA to transform the company in partnership with both the company's management and the World Bank. He agreed, so we took the proposition to Leon, who said: "Sounds terrific. Will the World Bank pay for it?" So Mario Leon, Doug Purvance, and I flew to Washington together to make our joint proposal to the World Bank. The World Bank agreed and approved the funding for the plan. Our focus in Brazil quickly shifted to working with COSIPA to execute a turnaround and building of a major steel company. Over the next several years, COSIPA effectively completed the World Bank–financed expansion, became a successful, profitable steel producer, and paid back its obligations to the World Bank.

The major ingredients for a successful turnaround are (1) a sound plan, (2) a capable management team committed to the success of the plan, and (3) the necessary skills and funds to execute the plan. Our job was to create the plan, get management's buy-in, identify the necessary skills to implement the plan, and assist in managing the transformation process. We worked in every area of the company in partnership with managers from the top to the bottom of the organization.

When facing a new and unfamiliar challenge, draw deeply on all of your experiences and supplement them with wise and experienced partners. Your best tools are listening, questioning, and understanding.

State-owned enterprises are effective means of launching or improving a country's position in an industry, but government ownership impedes innovation and development of management and processes necessary for industry leadership in free markets.

EXPANDING IN BRAZIL

My involvement in the business community started with a trip with a group of Brazilian executives to Forteleza in the northeast of Brazil to learn about the economic developments there. Fortunately, I was welcomed on the four-day study tour, and most of the participants spoke English. Several of them became good friends over our time in Brazil. We joined a Brazilian country club instead of the international club, which had mostly expatriate members. Week by week my network expanded.

Once the COSIPA project was launched, we began building a local professional staff of Brazilians with a good education, intelligence, and a zest for hard and challenging work. During the next two and a half years on the wings of an expanding economy, we worked with a mix of state-owned enterprises, private-sector Brazilian companies, and a few subsidiaries of U.S. and other foreign corporations. New clients came from recommendations by current clients and their boards and relationships developed in the community. The staff grew to fifty professionals, all but a few of them Brazilian. Several ultimately became partners, and one, Oscar Bernardes, became head of the Brazilian office and a director of Booz Allen, and ultimately a CEO of a global agribusiness company. Importantly, word of the success of our clients spread in the business community, and our phone began to ring.

I will describe our work with two clients: BNDE, the National Bank for Economic Development; and Indústrias Villares, a private-sector manufacturing company. BNDE is included because of its importance to the Brazilian economy. Villares is included as an example of a sophisticated and successful player in the expanding private sector.

BNDE

Marcos Vianna was the newly appointed president of BNDE. The government-owned bank was founded in 1952 to be the primary source of capital formation in the country, both equity capital and long-term loans. BNDE had been around for twenty years, but Vianna thought it was under-serving the country and the economy. He wanted it to be a major engine for growth in Brazil. Someone told him he should talk with Booz Allen. I flew to Rio to meet him a few days later.

Vianna was an intense, athletic, energetic young man about thirty-two years old, who looked like Omar Sharif. He came right to the point: "BNDE isn't doing a fraction of what it should for this country." The loan portfolio was focused on SOEs and infrastructure projects and hadn't grown with the economy or reached out to other segments of the economy that had potential for growth. He spent the next two hours describing the situation as he saw it, answering all my questions. He then sat back and said, "There you have it. Do you think you can help?"

We spent another full hour discussing what the bank might be doing differently. I was taken by the clarity of his vision, the depth of his analysis of the business, and his ability to articulate his thinking perfectly in heavily accented English. I thought this man might be president of Brazil one day, an idea that became more credible the more I got to know him. He wanted to move quickly. BNDE was an essential link to the growth and success of corporate Brazil—and therefore of the country. BNDE was an ideal company to work with. It was at the center of Brazil's growth plan. Its new CEO was committed to change whatever was necessary to succeed in its mission and was open to outside help. I was convinced that we could help.

I delivered the letter a week after our first meeting. He read it carefully, pushed his chair back, and said, "Can you start today?" Weeks later, I asked Vianna how he came to his decision so quickly. His reply, "You understood my problem and what I wanted to achieve."

Understanding is one of the most important things a consultant brings to a client and is an essential first step in developing mutual trust.

We asked Larry Wilsey, a senior partner in Chicago with extensive organization and government experience, to take on the project with me. After about three weeks, Wilsey came up with an unorthodox organization concept that Vianna loved. He laid out the organization of the Catholic Church with God at the top as chairman surrounded by his angel-directors, the pope as CEO, and various departments run by cardinals as EVPs. The mission was to spread God's word, make converts to the Church, establish rules (doctrine) to manage behavior and reward performance of the clergy and faithful, and to engage in fundraising. In his oral presentation he drew the links with BNDE's mission and operations. This framework enabled Vianna and his team to think totally differently about the bank and its organization. The basic mission of both the Church and BNDE was the same: growth, service, and fundraising. It raised its sights to the strategic goals of the institution rather than thinking about incremental improvements to the existing organization. It also made the project fun for everyone. Nobody missed a meeting. Everyone came with fresh ideas.

We agreed on a new mission statement for BNDE that reflected its more expansive role and ambition, a strategy for the country in capital formation, BNDE's role in executing that strategy, and the organization, staffing, and systems necessary to carry it out. The mission was to evolve as the economy grew and Brazil's economic policy evolved. Provisions were made for adding new departments and subsidiaries as the financing requirements of the country's major economic players changed and expanded. While infrastructure and import substitution were the main goals of the government at the time, we envisioned changes in that mission and built in the flexibility to support new government and private-sector policies and initiatives. History has borne out the wisdom of that decision, as BNDE financing has expanded by multiples, and it took on the mission of social development in addition to its original economic development mission. Also BNDE became profitable.

We worked with Vianna on implementing these plans. BNDE's star rose in Brazil as it became an essential link in financing Brazil's growth. Marketing was far less important because state-owned and private corporations and entrepreneurs beat on BNDE's doors for financial help. Marcos Vianna became a major player in the financial sector and a trusted political advisor.

BNDES, as it is now called, has remained the most important enabler of capital formation in Brazil over forty years later. Its role has expanded as the economy has grown in size, complexity, and global involvement. Today BNDES is the second-largest national development bank in the world (China's is first) with total assets of $270 billion and loans of almost $200 billion. It is larger than the World Bank.

Dream Big. Marcos Vianna showed me the value of aiming beyond what everyone expected for his organization. He envisioned a role for BNDE orders of magnitude greater than it had previously achieved.

INDÚSTRIAS VILLARES

We studied the private sector to identify companies that could benefit from our help. On top of our list was Indústrias Villares, a privately owned manufacturing company, large by Brazilian standards, located in São Paulo. Villares was the model enterprise for the country's import substitution policy. Their products included specialty steel, automotive parts, elevators, and a number of other industrial products. They had several technical alliances with foreign firms. They appeared well-positioned to take advantage of the robust economy. I contacted the chairman and founder, Luiz Dumont Villares, introduced myself, and asked for a meeting.

Mr. Villares explained that he was handing over the management of the firm to his son, Paulo, and suggested I call him. Interestingly, Villares' uncle, Alberto Santos-Dumont, flew an airplane outside Paris in 1906, which Brazilians consider was the first successful manned flight entirely under its own power—and therefore Santos-Dumont was the rightful "father of aviation." The airport in São Paulo is named Santos-Dumont.

Paulo Villares was in his early thirties, flawless English, intense, well-versed in the company's businesses, brimming with ideas. He reminded me in many ways of Marcos Vianna. We hit it off well immediately. Paulo was an avid reader of the latest business books and wanted to try out almost every new idea. We began by discussing his aspirations for the company and moved into specific issues within each of his businesses. Over time, we did several projects for his company—cost reduction, reorganization, evaluations of new investments, industry strategies—but much of our time together was spent discussing ideas about his businesses, his organization and people, and plans for the future. I became his sounding board and counselor. Villares became one of my most interesting clients in Brazil.

One of his concerns was the union situation in an industrial area outside São Paulo where his auto parts plants were located. The union leader, Luiz Inácio Lula da Silva, was fomenting unrest among Villares employees and making demands beyond the company's ability to meet them. Lula, as he was commonly called, subsequently entered politics and was elected president of Brazil from 2003 to 2011. You never know with whom you are dealing.

Paulo and I worked together for eighteen months until my family and I moved to Paris. The company grew rapidly and generated strong returns. Indústrias Villares was in good hands with CEO Paulo Villares.

Experiences early in your career will reappear later on a bigger stage. Remember the Jasper Saw Company?

We moved a few experienced professionals to Brazil. Newt Parks, a senior partner who helped establish Booz Allen in Europe, was nearing retirement. Newt was looking for another challenge, and we agreed he would be a great fit for Brazil. He joined us to open a Rio office. Newt, Barbara, and their seven Yorkies became stars in the Rio social circles, and he built an excellent clientele in the robust private sector of local and international firms. Another example, Paul Kaestle, a partner with whom I had worked extensively in Chicago, came to back me up until we had enough local partners . . . and in the event that I would leave Brazil. When I moved to Paris, Kaestle became head of the office and remained there until a Brazilian, Oscar Bernardes, was ready to take over. The office flourished for several years.

Seek help. Most successful business leaders seek out the best talent they can find and recognize that the team with the best players almost always wins.

Do not become indispensable in any one position. Always have a good replacement available so you can be mobile professionally.

Brazil became one of the best performing units in the firm. Our clients were thriving and satisfied and growing in number. Our staff was growing in size and talent. We were very profitable. We had become an important firm in Brazil. In early 1974, we hosted Jim Farley, the new CEO of Booz Allen, and our new vice-chairman, Harry Vincent, in Rio and São Paulo. Harry took me aside and told me they wanted me to move to Paris and work with John Rhodes to run the firm's international business. Rhodes was my boss, close friend, and partner . . . and became one of my most important mentors. I had figured out that my weakest area was building senior relationships with executives who weren't yet clients, and Rhodes was superb at it. An excellent match.

Seek out mentors who can and are willing to teach you their craft.

FRANCE

My role and activities as president of Booz Allen International were much different from the predominantly client work I had up till then. In Chicago and São Paulo, my clients were relatively nearby—either a cab ride or a short flight away. Living in Paris with responsibility for offices in Asia, South America, Africa, and the Middle East, however, meant that my clients could be on other continents. We had to have qualified professionals in those countries to work directly with the clients.

My primary job was to build the firm's presence outside North America and Europe, which meant deciding where to go and which clients to pursue, and building on-site teams. Our aspiration was to make good management as important as good politics and good economics in our host countries. Our goal was to be the leading management consulting firm on those continents. My initial task was to understand what we had in place, which countries/markets we should target, and then to create a plan for moving forward. In my mind I was the firm's missionary to bring our gospel of good management to countries whose conditions appeared to be receptive to our message.

Historically, outside the US and Europe, the firm had worked with clients that had World Bank–funded projects. The clients were typically government agencies or SOEs. The firm did little to expand to other industries or the private sector in these locations. Our first major break with that tradition was in South America, particularly in Brazil. We searched for more opportunities like Brazil—robust economy, ambition to grow and improve, openness to foreign firms like ours, a capitalist economic system (sort of), and not hostile to the United States.

We identified about twenty countries outside North America and Europe as potential markets for Booz Allen. We picked ten as our initial target list based on our assessment of potential to build a multi-client practice within the next decade. Each had a diverse economy and aspirations to expand their economies both domestically and globally. We had offices in three—Japan, Brazil, and Venezuela. The others were Iran, Argentina, Chile, South Africa, Australia, the United Arab Emirates (UAE), and Hong Kong. These countries all appeared suitable to growing a broad client base that could benefit from our services. And offices in those countries could service nearby markets.

The other nine had longer-term potential—China, Russia, Saudi Arabia, Algeria, India, Morocco, Taiwan, South Korea, and Thailand—clearly not ready then but almost certain to become major markets in the future. At that time the U.S. was locked in a cold war with Russia, and China had just been "opened" by Nixon and Kissinger.

A clear roadmap based on solid rationale and objective analysis is important before you rush out the door.

We developed a strategy for expanding our practice in each of the top-ten countries and agreed that if a large project came up in one of the other ten, we would consider pursuing it. We had project offices in two of the other ten—Thailand and Algeria. We recognized that our resources were limited and that our best course was to build our current positions and invest discretionary time on priority countries. It was clear that our priorities would likely change with shifting geopolitical currents and opportunities.

We created an international headquarters in Paris that would provide services for all of the firm's international activities, including Europe. Rhodes believed that the English Channel became wider than the Atlantic Ocean for American firms that established international headquarters in London. Our family moved to Paris that summer. Boris Bruz, a senior partner resident in Paris, took over the European business.

The first month on any new job is crucial. Put the most important things at the top of your list. In this case it was mission and strategy.

My first three years in Paris were devoted to the world outside North America and Europe. Ralph Smiley, Booz Allen's pioneer internationally, was about to retire. Ralph and I set out on a grand tour to introduce me as his successor. Over the next few months we visited many of the countries on our target list, plus a few others that he knew well. Smiley was greeted like a revered guru everywhere.

The decision was clear for Argentina and Chile: Set up an office in Buenos Aires and serve Chile from that base with an assist to both from Brazil. Australia was another obvious target. They had a real democracy and free-market capitalism . . . and they spoke English. The biggest obstacle was distance and the difficulty of sending temporary resources to support client teams. Nevertheless, Sydney became a successful practice with a broad clientele. John Prescott, CEO of Broken Hill Proprietary, became our largest client and then a member of our International Advisory Board. The firm had worked for years in South Africa and Hong Kong. Hong-Kong Shanghai Bank (HSBC) was a long-term client. We decided that near term we would continue to serve them from afar. I continued to be active with clients in Brazil and Venezuela.

My building efforts were devoted to Abu Dhabi, Tokyo, and Tehran during my years as head of Booz Allen International. Tokyo and Tehran are briefly described here.

JAPAN

The firm had an office in Tokyo for some years without much traction. Rhodes and I concluded that our philosophy of management was close to the Japanese and could be well received. There were no Japanese or international competitors in general management consulting, although there was a consulting industry in technology, market research, and specialized systems. We needed to amp up our commitment. Japan became a priority.

Japan had been rebuilt from the ashes of World War II and was thriving both domestically and internationally through exports to many world markets, including the U.S. Japan had a capitalist economy with major government support. The companies involved in exports—e.g., autos, shipbuilding, farm and construction machinery, chemicals, consumer electronics, and a number of other industrial products—were referred to as "Japan, Inc." because of the close coordination and support by the government in the export markets.

We believed that we could add value to Japanese companies with our approach to management. Japan is a closed society by Western standards. Japanese are suspicious of foreigners—foreign firms or investment were not welcomed. We believed that a partnership with a highly respected Japanese company would give us the imprimatur necessary for local acceptance. The top executives at Dai-Ichi Kangyo Bank (DKB) agreed.

We formed a joint venture with the DKB, the largest bank in Japan, in 1975. On my quarterly visits to Tokyo, the president of DKB would host grand lunches with a roomful of his top management team and would tell the group that DKB-Booz Allen Consulting would become the most important consulting firm in the country and would help Japanese companies become the most efficient in the world. His timeframe was fifty years, which underscored a major difference in the perspectives of Japanese and American business leaders. We decided to expand our office.

DAIEI INC.

One good example of a client relationship in Japan was Daiei, the largest supermarket chain in the country. We were introduced to Daiei by DKB. We asked Bill Monroe (who had taken a younger me on his team working with Allis-Chalmers) to work with Daiei. Monroe had several supermarket and department store clients in the U.S. Daiei, a successful company in Japan, was an excellent test case of our approach to management. The founder, owner, and CEO, Isao Nakauchi, was in the midst of a major expansion into department stores. In addition, he was concerned because, while the company had grown significantly, profitability was below his expectations. The small owner-run stores his company was replacing were not going quietly. Daiei was outside the umbrella of Japan, Inc., and operated in a free-market environment, so there was no government help for him.

In fact, most people sided emotionally and culturally with the little guys. Monroe understood the problem and went to work identifying the cost-and-profit-improvement levers used by supermarkets and department stores in the U.S. He introduced concepts that were effective in marketing and managing supermarkets in the U.S. The goal was to make the consumer experience—price, quality, and breadth of products—so compelling that consumers would switch to Daiei. He and his team identified significant cost-reduction opportunities. He counseled with Nakauchi on how to integrate his department store acquisitions and recommended a new organization structure for managing the diversified businesses. Monroe spent hours debating with Nakauchi on his ambitious diversification program. Profits rose quickly. Nakauchi was delighted and became our best advocate. Over the next two decades, Daiei continued to grow and diversify and was ranked in the top twenty retailers in the world.

We learned a lot about Japanese traditions and management practices. A number of practices that were common in the U.S. had not been employed in Japan, and vice versa. Japanese companies were highly centralized. Major decisions were rarely delegated down the line. There were few profit centers at lower levels. Strategy was the responsibility of the CEO and a few close advisors. Rarely did companies seek outside advice on strategy or organization. Daiei was a breakthrough.

On the other hand, Japanese companies employed a bottom-up approach in production and developed excellent new techniques in manufacturing and quality control, which have since been employed in the U.S. and Europe. Japan was also a leader in statistical analysis, lean manufacturing, and factory floor quality control. I had no doubt that they would become a factor in the global auto industry. The *zaibatsu* was a unique Japanese organization concept with alliances among diverse companies that supported one another, particularly in export markets.

To learn more about U.S./Japan issues and to build relationships, I joined the U.S.-Japan Business Council, an organization of chairmen and CEOs of large companies from both countries. Meetings were substantive, and I got to know top executives from several Japanese companies. A highlight was making a speech at a meeting in Tokyo on direct foreign investment. Japan needed to open up to foreign investment and competition. The response of the Japanese was predictably inscrutable.

The cultural differences between Japan and the U.S. pervade all areas of business and personal life. Tradition, formality, hierarchy, respect for age and position, and the role of the family are all much more important in Japan. While Japan has been changing in many ways since the Second World War, cultural change has progressed slowly. Japan's business class is well-educated, smart, clever, intensely hard-working and competitive . . . and very male.

Over the next decade the firm expanded its clientele to a number of important Japanese companies, working with both their domestic and international operations. Unquestionably we learned as much as we taught. The combination of U.S. and Japanese approaches to managing business has powerful potential. U.S. companies have adopted many Japanese manufacturing practices. Japan revolutionized automotive design and manufacturing. We introduced new approaches to strategy, organization, cost control, and marketing into Japan's playbook. We never figured out how to transport the zaibatsu concept to America.

In the past twenty years, Japan has struggled economically as its wages rose and countries like China, India, and Korea undercut Japan as a low-cost manufacturing location. Japan's resistance to direct foreign investment has deprived it of both investment dollars and access to technologies. Japan's growth slowed to a crawl for over two decades. Despite its stagnant economy, there is very low inflation and unemployment; Japan is still the third-largest economy in the world at $5 trillion GDP and competes effectively in global markets in a number of industries.

In building a business, have patience. A country like Japan measures progress in generations, not quarterly results. Trust-based relationships, which are crucial in business, should be built to last.

IRAN

When I took my world tour with Ralph Smiley in 1974, Tehran was a major stop. Smiley's relationships dated back to the revolution that put the Shah back on the throne in the 1950s. Smiley led the project to reorganize the National Iranian Oil Company in 1958. All doors were open to Ralph. He introduced me to former Deputy Prime Minister Shahbasi, an attorney who had in past years served as the firm's lawyer in Iran. I felt that Shahbasi would be perfect to introduce us to the business community. Shahbasi became our counselor in Iran.

Iran is thousands of years old. First recorded settlements date back to 7000 B.C. Persia, as it was called through most of its history, became the world's first global empire under Cyrus the Great in 550 B.C. At its peak, the Persian Empire controlled 40 percent of the world's population and straddled three continents. During the following two thousand years, competing empires—Roman, Byzantine, Ottoman, Russian—and invading nomadic tribes whittled away the Persian Empire, although it remained a nation with a cultural identity. Islam became the dominant religion by the tenth century. It became a monarchy in 1500, which lasted almost five centuries until 1979. Iranians have a proud heritage. They changed their name from Persia to Iran in 1935, but still refer to themselves as Persians (not Arabs).

In the mid-1970s, Iran was doing well economically, thanks principally to its oil exports; but the political scene was dangerous. The mullahs (Muslim clerics) had been calling for a revolution to oust the Shah for two decades. They wanted to transform Iran into an Islamic state, with the mullahs in charge under Sharia law—an Islamic theocracy.

Aside from the revolution being the primary topic of conversation, business continued as usual. We spent many evenings in the Tehran Hilton eating fresh pistachios and Iranian Imperial caviar while discussing both our client work and the revolution. Ayatollah Khomeini, the leader of the Islamic revolution in Iran, had been exiled in 1964, first to Turkey, then to Iraq, and finally to Paris in 1978 when the vice president of Iraq, Saddam Hussein, told Khomeini to leave Iraq, and France agreed to accept him. Khomeini reportedly controlled the revolution from his villa outside Paris.

A few months after our first meeting, Shahbasi asked if our firm would be interested in assisting Iran in upgrading its telecommunications system to world-class standards. AT&T would be our technical partner. The state of the telecom system was unreliable and primitive, comparable to pre-war America.

Our task was designing the strategy, the organization, and business systems necessary to run the Iranian Telecom Company. AT&T developed and implemented the technical architecture of the new system. We worked on the project until Ayatollah Khomeini returned to Iran. That project and another for Queen Farah Diba on population control, with the encouragement of Shahbasi, led us to conclude that we should open an office in Tehran. Doug Purvance, who had been elected partner while we were together in Brazil, agreed to head the office and develop a clientele. The firm's government business signed a technical assistance contract with the U.S. Air Force and the Iranian government for the F-16 fighter jet, which the U.S. was supplying to Iran. We were busy in Iran.

We found the management capabilities and business systems in both private and government-owned companies in Iran to be limited. Our gospel of mission, vision, and values followed by strategy, organization, and systems was exactly what Iran needed, but acceptance was tough. Iran's economy was a mix of government-controlled sectors and a highly fractured private sector of thousands of small and medium-sized companies. The influence of government was pervasive, and corruption was widespread. We worked with several companies and felt that given time we could have had a major impact on the Iranian economy.

It all came to a screeching halt in January 1979 when the revolution became violent. The Shah went into exile, and Ayatollah Khomeini returned from his exile in Paris on February 1. Iran was quickly turned into an Islamic state under Sharia law. Interestingly, our work and my travels in and out of the country were not affected by the revolution until Khomeini's return. In fact, Mitzi joined me for a week of travel through Iran, exploring the mosques and bazaars in Tehran and Isfahan a few months before the return of the Ayatollah.

When Ayatollah Khomeini returned, all Americans were told by the U.S. State Department to leave the country immediately. The U.S. Embassy in Tehran orchestrated the evacuation. Each individual was given a specific time and street corner to be picked up (with one suitcase) and taken to the airport for a designated flight to Western Europe. Shahbasi confirmed the gravity of the situation.

All of our employees got out safely, although one pressed his luck to the limit. When he arrived at the airport for his designated flight to Paris, he noticed another flight to Frankfurt was leaving a few hours later so he decided to stand by. His Paris flight left without him, and he was unable to take the Frankfurt flight, or any other flight. It took him more than a week to get out of Iran, accompanied by severe cases of angst within the U.S. Embassy and our firm. I spoke with him after his return and asked him what the %@#& he was thinking. He told me that everything seemed normal at the airport in Tehran and his girlfriend lived in Frankfurt, so why not switch flights just like in the U.S.? He was lucky he got out safely. A number of Iranians who supported the Shah were murdered, including Shahbasi's close friend, the prime minister. Fifty-two American hostages were held in the U.S. Embassy for 444 days. Booz Allen has never returned to Iran.

In international business, political risks are very important. Understand them. Take them seriously. And if the U.S. Embassy tells you to leave — leave!

EUROPE

About three years into our stay in Paris, my mandate expanded to include Europe—its business wasn't growing. The formula for success in management consulting was clear to me: Do outstanding work for every client on every assignment; build a team of the best professionals you can find and train them on the job with experienced partners; and get involved in the community to meet and work with CEOs who are potential clients. In each office, the leader was key.

With those rules in mind, Rhodes and I convinced Paul Anderson to move to Paris to lead the European practice. Anderson hired three new partners to strengthen our senior leadership, particularly in Germany, and sent Pierre Rodocanachi, a senior hire in Paris, to Cleveland to work with Jack McGrath to learn the consulting profession. It was a terrific investment. Pierre and his wife, Armande, returned soaked in Booz Allen culture. Pierre successfully led the French practice until he retired years later. We acquired Tage Bok Jennsen, a Danish consulting firm, and transferred several senior consultants from the U.S. to shore up our European staff. The European practice took off. Paul Anderson had brought the spark necessary to reignite our presence in Europe. My client work shifted to include Europe. British Leyland was the first. I enjoyed working with clients in the U.K., France, and Italy and was exhilarated by the upswing in the European business.

The team with the best players virtually always wins. Surround yourself with top talent.

THE BUYBACK OF THE FIRM

During my time in Paris, our board decided to buy back the firm from its public shareholders.

In the late 1960s, a number of the senior partners were reaching retirement, age sixty at that time. The bylaws required the firm to buy back their stock upon retirement. The firm had a board of partners, dubbed by the minions as the "Nine Old Men"—the most senior and longest-term partners, who owned over 70 percent of the firm's shares. The proposal was to go public and allow the retiring senior partners to sell shares at an initial public offering (IPO) and afterward in the open market. I must confess that when the partners voted on taking the firm public in 1969, I was a vocal advocate. My view was that buying back the stock of the nine old men would put a serious burden on the continuing partners. Rather, we should let them reap the payout they earned in building the firm by going public. It would then be up to us, the continuing partners, to take this extraordinary firm forward. In retrospect, going public was a terrible decision.

I misunderstood the debilitating effect on the partners of ceding 85 percent of the ownership to outsiders who were investors expecting a return. Partners became employees, not owners, which triggered a fundamental change in attitude. Arguably, we lost an entire generation of young partners who left the firm during the seven years of public ownership. Jim Farley, our new CEO, saw the effects on mindset and performance and began laying the groundwork for a buyback. The partners repurchased the firm in 1977. The buyback was financed by the firm's cash and a loan from the Continental Illinois Bank. This was one of the early leveraged buyouts by the management of a public company, a corporate strategy that became popular in the 1980s.

One of the major questions during that period was the form of governance the firm should adopt as a private company. When the firm was public, the directors were a mix of active partners and a few outside executives. I was asked to lead a small group of younger partners to come up with a new approach for governance. We took about six months interviewing most of our partners, understanding how other private professional firms worked, and developing options for governance as a private firm.

We recommended a governance system that was perilously close to democracy. A board of active partners was nominated by a governance committee chosen by the board. The partnership elected the new board. The board members had three-year, once-renewable, staggered terms and no additional compensation. The board was to reflect the composition of the partnership geographically, by business unit, tenure of partners, and diversity. The board had the normal authorities and responsibilities of boards of directors but also included the election of new partners and senior partners. We converted the Operating Council into a committee of senior partners. That governance system (documented in Booz Allen's renowned Green Book) remained in place without significant modification until the firm was sold thirty years later.

I served as chair of the Operating Council twice—first while in Paris and later after returning to the U.S. During my terms we dealt with a number of important and contentious issues, for example, determining the kind of firm we would be, going private, governance, major changes in the partner compensation system (big battles here), selling the firm (which had been discussed several times before actually doing it after I retired), establishing an advisory board, strategy, and succession.

One of the best decisions we made was to take the management role out of the compensation system and make pay dependent on professional performance. No longer would the head of an office or practice be the highest-paid partner in the unit, which enabled us to put younger partners in several management positions and keep senior partners full time with clients. The change also recognized the obvious—the highest rewards should go to those who contributed most to our primary mission, serving clients.

About twelve months later, Farley told me it was time to return to the U.S. We had revised the organization for the umpteenth time; I joined the firm's executive committee (called Farley's Cabinet), but remained focused administratively on the international business. My client work, however, shifted to the United States.

LESSONS ON CAPITALISM

During my eight years in Brazil and France, I had the opportunity to observe different forms of economic and political governance from the perspective of companies living and working under those regimes. The developed world had political democracies and capitalist economies. There were degree differences—forms of socialism and degrees of government control on the economic side. Most developing countries had significant government control over their economies and centralized political power—dictatorships, totalitarian regimes, quasi democracies.

In the developing world, important industries were either owned by the government—SOEs or government departments—or owned by wealthy families, often over several generations. Efficiency, modern management practices, and ethics were undervalued. The missions of the SOEs typically included activities that belong to the government in democracies, such as social programs, guaranteed employment, healthcare, and other political objectives. Boards and managers were chosen from political supporters, friends of the ruler, and the "aristocracy." SOEs are virtually all monopolies and don't have to respond to market and competitive forces. Under those systems, there are inadequate incentives to innovate, improve efficiency, or invest in projects that are not politically supported regardless of their market or economic attractiveness. Political goals and keeping rulers in power dominate policy and funding of SOEs.

Few developing countries have become developed countries in the last century. Chile, Singapore, and South Korea are three that have. They all adopted free-market capitalism. Other countries slipped backward from developed economies to developing—such as Argentina, East Germany, and Czechoslovakia, which adopted socialism over capitalism. The oil-rich countries of the Middle East and Venezuela have not adopted free-market capitalism and still suffer as developing economies despite their wealth.

I continue to hope that Brazil will make the transition to free-market capitalism. Brazil would have progressed significantly further and faster if it had spun off many of its SOEs into the private sector and reduced regulation dramatically. Brazil has the natural resources and plenty of spirited and capable entrepreneurs to become an independent economic powerhouse.

Most developing countries protected local industries with trade barriers that have the adverse effect of slowing the progress of local firms toward becoming efficient or technically advanced enough to compete either with importers or as an exporter.

In its purest form, free-market capitalism allocates funds to companies that are the most efficient and whose products and services are most successful in the market. The best-funded companies can invest more in new products, new technologies, and modern manufacturing and marketing processes. Free-market competition forces innovation. If a company fails to meet the needs of its customers, its competitors will. Capitalism enables the accumulation of wealth, even great wealth, by companies and individuals. It provides incentives and rewards to those who innovate, take risks, and serve markets well.

On my first trip to China in 1983, we found that the government had discovered that many farmers were working their fields after delivering the mandatory production required by the government. The farmers were selling the extra production to the townspeople at prices well below government-set levels and pocketing the revenue. Production per hour was substantially higher during those "off" hours. Rather than clamp down on this tiny but successful free market, Deng Xiaoping, China's leader, allowed the diversion from communist orthodoxy of agricultural communes to continue without explicitly approving it. Deng quietly allowed similar moves into the free market in several other industries. The result has been an extraordinary transformation of almost half the Chinese economy toward a form of capitalism, which continues today. The regulations on these companies are often severe, but many entrepreneurs have become fabulously wealthy.

Under Deng, China opened to foreign investment—though with significant strings attached. Foreign investors were required to have Chinese partners with majority control. China used this control to gain access to foreign technology, typically without compensation. Nevertheless, the lure of the enormous potential market in China and very low labor costs was irresistible to large numbers of foreign corporations wishing to build plants and establish bases in China. Apple and Nike, for example, outsourced most of their manufacturing to China. Consequently, China has maintained its political control while allowing capitalism in the country.

Many Chinese SOEs continue to exist and to be models of inefficiency—burdened with supplying jobs, pensions, healthcare, housing, and education for large numbers of people who would otherwise be unemployed or uncared for by the state. State banks are required to grant loans to SOEs, which free-market banks would never approve, to assure the continued operation of the SOEs. The Chinese experiment with capitalism has transformed China. China's GDP has shown high growth rates as its billion-plus population migrates from farms to urban communities. Chinese "capitalism" can be credited for raising several hundred million people out of poverty and starvation, in stark contrast to the results of the socialist/communist experiments of Mao.

When the America China Society was meeting with President Jiang Zemin in the mid-1990s, we asked him when China would open its political and economic system. His response: "We are moving slowly to capitalism but will retain political control through the Communist Party until the time is right to open the political process." He added that attempting to open both at the same time is foolish, as the Russian experiment proved. The president of China confirmed his country's view that capitalism was superior to communism and socialism. The Chinese experiment is one of the best examples of the power of capitalism to lift a nation out of poverty and into the competitive world. If China were to privatize its SOEs and embrace capitalism throughout its economy, watch out USA.

Capitalism is not without its faults. Unfettered capitalism can take advantage of its workers, allow pollution of the environment, create monopolies, unjustly enrich its corporate owners, and permit actions harmful to the common good. Capitalism requires regulations that control behaviors detrimental to society. Laissez-faire capitalism, which Adam Smith proposed in his seminal *Wealth of Nations,* dictates no government intervention and doesn't protect society's interests. All democratic governments have adopted protections. The trick is to achieve the proper balance of regulations that protect society without killing the spirit that capitalism breeds and deliver the living standards every society strives to achieve.

REFLECTION

Our experience in Brazil and France both professionally and for the family was superb. On the professional side, I had the opportunity to work in twenty-plus countries with over forty client organizations in several different industries at a time when the world was locked in the Cold War and developing countries were shifting toward democracy. Signs of the globalization of the world's economy were sprouting everywhere. NATO was strong; OPEC rose up, dramatically changing the

Middle East. South America was bustling; Asia had shaken off the tragedy of the Second World War and was leaning westward.

Our gospel that "good management enables prosperity" was proven almost everywhere we worked. While the U.S. certainly did not have all the secrets to effective corporate management, U.S. management consulting firms did spread the gospel and practice of good management principles throughout the world. Personally, I was part of the transformation of a number of important enterprises and witnessed the positive impact they had on their national economies. My understanding of business, management, and diverse customs and cultures grew substantially. I had the privilege of working with so many extraordinary people. It was clear that no country has a monopoly on talent or ideas. I learned from them all. Like my family, I would never trade these experiences for a more ordered life in one place.

LESSONS LEARNED

My first and probably most important lesson was an understanding and appreciation of different cultures and ways of life. Throughout history, many civilizations have contributed vitally to the advancement of the human race—in science, philosophy, religion, knowledge, and how to work together to achieve vastly more than individuals working alone can. What we have today is accumulation of the knowledge and wisdom of past generations and civilizations. The best we can hope to say about our own contributions is that the world is a better place because of what our generation or our civilization did. We owe our place in history to our forebears, and we have an obligation to our children and grandchildren and all who follow to make their lives better. It is necessary to understand history and the achievements of others to understand today and to imagine tomorrow with any accuracy.

Chapter Six

BACK IN THE USA

The transition back to the U.S. was relatively easy professionally, although the family would have been happy staying in Paris. This chapter lasted twenty-three years and presents activities and decisions made during some of the most productive years of my career. Those activities and decisions are discussed here to give young professionals a picture and sense of life as a senior management consultant.

Within weeks after we got back to the U.S., Farley got the call from Treasury Secretary Miller to help Chrysler. And off I went, as detailed in chapter one. Chrysler absorbed the majority of my time and energy for several months.

AT&T

A short time later, we were asked by AT&T to help them develop a strategy for taking Ma Bell overseas. AT&T had given technical assistance to companies and governments outside the U.S., but had no international operations. Almost all countries had national telephone companies that were predominantly state-owned. With the state of technology at that time, the hurdles in establishing telephone services outside a home country were considerable to insurmountable. The principal benefit of the project for AT&T was to shift its vision from one domestic market to the world market, which was just around the corner. We had worked with AT&T in Iran (see chapter five) and a number of times in the U.S.

Initial steps taken by AT&T internationally were limited—strengthening relations with national companies, expanded long distance service, gearing up an international staff to actively expand alliances—but the direction was clear. AT&T intended to become a global telecommunications company. And its successor companies are all global.

It reminded me of our project with AT&T in the 1960s to develop a marketing strategy. At that time AT&T did no marketing and limited planning for new products and services. We had recommended a significant change in policy toward marketing and product/service development. AT&T moved slowly but powerfully through the water. They were careful to a fault, but very effective once they decided on their direction. I later returned to AT&T to assist one of the senior executives, Jerre Stead, CEO of AT&T Global Solutions (formerly NCR Corporation, which AT&T had recently acquired), in making his business more competitively nimble. Unlike the early leaders in most industries transformed by radical changes in technology, AT&T has survived and thrived. Regulatory protection played a part, but the tradition of strong management development was probably the most important reason for its success. The telecommunications industry has been turned upside down in the last thirty years with the cell phone, the internet, the iPhone, and social media. Shortly after our work, the government broke AT&T into seven operating companies, dubbed the Baby Bells, AT&T long distance, and Lucent Technologies (formerly Western Electric Co.). All have continued to adapt through mergers and creating new businesses, including merging with one another. All operate internationally. All are profitable and growing. A key characteristic of the AT&T culture still exists in its offspring—move slowly and cautiously to understand risks and opportunities, but once you decide, move aggressively. AT&T and its successor companies navigated one of the biggest transformations in industrial history and survived.

Caution is not always bad, particularly in a highly volatile environment.

NEXT STOP: CHICAGO

After only eighteen months in New York, I was asked by Farley to move again, this time to Chicago to take over the Midwest for the firm. The firm's need in Chicago was compelling, and I was ready to get off the multi-continent milk run.

Chicago was my first real opportunity to create a long-term clientele in my hometown. My task was to build a network of relationships and demonstrate to the business leaders in Chicago that Booz Allen could be a great partner to work with. The firm had a long and successful run in Chicago, but was beginning to fall behind. Mitzi and I were both natives of Chicago and, as a result, had family and friends there—a big plus. However, it had been ten years since we moved to Brazil, so we were really starting over to make a new life.

We believed that the best way to build a satisfying social and professional life in Chicago was to dive into the community. The decision to become actively involved in the community was a major factor in any success I enjoyed for the rest of my career in consulting. Through community boards and projects, I met and became friends with most of the business leaders in Chicago and built a substantial network.

Life outside the office may be more important and productive than life in the office.

BOOZ ALLEN & HAMILTON

Chicago was the birthplace of Booz Allen Hamilton sixty-seven years before. Ed Booz, Jim Allen, and Carl Hamilton were all Chicagoans. They were pioneers in an entirely new industry. Booz set up shop in 1914, offering business surveys to companies. A psychologist, Booz also conducted interviews of executives to assess their suitability and potential to be managers and leaders. Jim Allen joined Booz in 1929 with the idea of expanding its vision from a small firm of individuals to a professional management consulting firm addressing a broader range of management issues with a larger clientele. Carl Hamilton joined as a partner in 1935. Many of the consulting firms established in the next forty years were started by partners and staff from Booz Allen.

By the mid-1960s when I joined, Booz Allen was a brand name for large corporations in the U.S. and Europe. But it was still small—$38 million in revenue, according to a *BusinessWeek* cover story on the firm in the late 1960s. In the following fifteen years, management consulting grew dramatically, as did Booz Allen. New York and Washington surpassed Chicago as the largest offices in the firm. My job was to accelerate growth in the Midwest.

My first task was to get involved with clients and in the community. United Airlines and Amoco Corporation became two of my most important clients. I will describe my work with them because they are good examples of the changes occurring in their important industries. Both were at inflection points. United was wrestling with the effects of deregulation of its industry. Both United and Amoco were heavily impacted by the large swings in oil prices after the OPEC crisis in 1973.

UNITED AIRLINES

In 1982, Dick Ferris, the CEO of United Airlines, asked my former partner in Chicago, Doug Petrie, for a recommendation of a consultant to help him redirect United to compete more effectively in the post-regulated airline industry. Petrie gave him my name. Ferris was an aviation buff and loved flying. His executive experience, however, was with hotels, not airlines. He joined United in 1971 as head of food service for Westin Hotels, which United had purchased a year earlier. He became CEO of United in 1979. Ferris had a well-earned reputation of being smart, decisive, tough, and competitive. He was committed to beating his arch-rival American Airlines on every metric in the book. The matchup between Dick Ferris at United and Bob Crandall at American was epic.

The biggest issue facing United's airline business in 1982, in Ferris's mind, was its failure to make the transition from its regulated environment to the competitive world after Congress passed the Airline Deregulation Act in 1978. During the regulated period, the Civil Aeronautics Board controlled fares and routes. Airlines spent most of their muscle securing routes and fare increases in Washington. The deregulation law freed routes and prices from government control. U.S. airlines could fly anywhere and charge anything. The competitive game was on.

Both regulation and deregulation have tremendous business consequences and require swift, continuous, and unique responses.

Airlines took quick actions to secure their principal hub cities. American led the pack in introducing clever marketing like its frequent flier program, AAdvantage, which others scrambled to replicate. American also modified its automated reservation system, Sabre, which was used by travel agents for all airlines, to give American flights preferential display. This resulted in higher selection of its flights by travel agents. While the courts later ruled bias in display illegal, these actions demonstrated the competitive fever that followed deregulation. American was the first to establish alliances with international carriers to provide a seamless flight experience across the world. The One World alliance has eleven full members and another dozen airlines with commercial agreements.

Ferris wanted United to become a nimble, lower-cost company with a fierce competitive spirit. He had a carload of ideas—like turning the organization upside down with the customer at the top, cutting fixed costs by 30 percent, and creating a partnership with the unions to reverse years of combat. We spent the first few weeks understanding the competitive levers in the post-regulatory world, their value to customers and the airline, and how these levers could be turned in United's favor. United had a lot of catching up to do.

There was consensus that the organization had to be more focused on the customer and that costs had to be much lower. Price had already become a competitive weapon. In a price-competitive market, the low-cost producer wins. On the other hand, consumers had choices and wanted flights going where they wanted, when they wanted, with as little hassle and as much comfort as possible. Cost reduction became the first order of business. Ferris created the "gang of four," which he borrowed from the Cultural Revolution–era insurgents in China. His gang of four were United's top executives, who would devote a large chunk of their time figuring out how to reduce costs substantially while retaining competitiveness on customer-facing activities . . . and then get it done. Booz Allen was United's staff on the project. Everything was on the table, no sacred cows. To prove it, our first visits were to the Maintenance Center in San Francisco, a no-fly zone for so-called "infidels" (members of United organizations outside Maintenance). We worked together for over two years across the company, and the costs came down substantially. It should be noted that maintenance costs did come down, but carefully, with no risks to safety. Throughout the company the organizations were changed and levels were eliminated; every activity was questioned and a lot were dropped; stations were refocused and many eliminated; the revered maintenance department was restructured; routes and fares were analyzed and adjusted through the prism of profitability; new systems and reporting metrics were implemented; and people were evaluated for their ability to compete in an unregulated industry.

To enhance customer experience, a goal was set to get the customer from the airport curb to the door of the plane with zero delays—the check-in process was a nightmare at busy times in the morning and late afternoon. (It took about twenty years and major new technology to allow self-check-in . . . and then along came security screening post-9/11.) Everything—yes, everything—was changed. United came out of the 1982 recession a stronger, more profitable company. Most important, the attitude and spirit in the company reflected Ferris's competitiveness.

For Ferris, the job of being the best in the industry was never done. He bought Pan Am's Asian business in one of the most significant acquisitions in the industry up to that date. Again we acted as the staff to plan and implement the integration of Pan Am's operations into United. While there were problems with engines on Pan Am's Lockheed L-1011 fleet, the acquisition was well managed and established United as a leader in the transpacific market, which proved to be a savior for the airline a decade later.

Ferris had long had a dream of transforming United into a travel behemoth that would offer full travel services to corporate and individual customers. He bought Hertz Rent-a-Car and Hilton International Hotels, which was paired with United's Westin Group to become one of the largest hotel companies in the world. He changed the name of the parent company from United to Allegis, which was widely ridiculed.

During that time, the company was embroiled in a damaging strike with the pilot's union.

Good customer service had long been the holy grail for airlines and equally as difficult to attain. Cost competitiveness was now also a top priority. The trick was to achieve both.

Rebranding is tricky. Anybody remember Allegis?

In addition to the normal economic issues, the Air Line Pilots Association (ALPA) was upset that Ferris was spending money on hotels and car rental companies rather than airplanes. The union gained support from investors, particularly Coniston Partners, and some board members who opposed the diversification. The strike was settled, but shortly after, the union made a bid to acquire the company and spin off the hotels and Hertz. The first bid failed, but the drama cost Ferris his job. Frank Olson, the long-time CEO of Hertz, became acting CEO of Allegis in June 1987.

Steve Wolf was hired as the new CEO in December 1987. A few months later, the company sold most of its non-airline businesses and changed its name to UAL, emphasizing that its core was an airline.

We worked closely with Wolf and his team on a number of projects. One of the most interesting was an analysis of the airline industry since deregulation for UAL's board. The industry had gone through several periods of rapid expansion and profitability, each followed by a recession that had resulted cumulatively in zero profits for the industry during deregulation from 1979 to 1993. During that time the industry had invested billions in new equipment and facilities. As representatives of the shareholders, what should the board do? How, for example, could UAL avoid the damaging fluctuation in earnings? How should it plan capacity growth? Should its current footprint in the U.S. be altered? Was the airline big and broad enough to serve the needs of its important business customers? Should it merge with another airline?

The economics of the airline business were fairly simple, but managing an airline was very complex. First the economics:

1. If you own or lease a plane, keep it flying. The ownership costs dwarf the operating costs of a plane.
2. If you have an empty seat, fill it. The incremental cost of a passenger was very low, so the extra passenger became profitable at almost any fare.
3. Put your planes on your busiest and highest-yield routes. As a result, high-volume routes became heavily competitive, and low-volume routes were often underserved.

With these economics, airlines seldom grounded aircraft voluntarily to reduce capacity. Industry overcapacity stayed around until the number of passengers rose to fill the planes. When the industry had too much capacity, airlines strived to fill seats by reducing fares rather than grounding planes. The economics of an empty seat drove airlines to compete on fares, and fare wars had become common in the post-regulation years. Once an airline reduced price on a route, its competitors responded quickly.

It seemed foolish to start a fare war, but they were common. The temptation to grab share was overwhelming, particularly for low-cost airlines that thought they could win a price war. The majors, however, had lots of routes and dropped prices on specific routes where necessary to match competitors. The pricing game became very sophisticated. Airlines made major investments to improve their pricing models, which became a key competitive tool. An interesting dilemma was that, while it paid the airline to fill the last seat at any price, the bulk of last-minute fliers were on business and less sensitive to price. The airlines learned to charge full price for last-minute fliers. In fact, most airlines today believe that the last seats sold determine the profitability of the flight.

These dynamics, along with rising and falling oil prices, resulted in major losses during recessions. It is not an overstatement to say that the entire industry has teetered on bankruptcy in every major recession since deregulation. When the economy was strong, passenger demand rose, seats filled, capacity tightened, and profits rose. In response, airlines increased capacity and unions demanded more pay to share in the success. As the boom matured and another recession loomed, demand softened, and prices began to fall to fill seats. This cycle repeated almost congruently with the economic cycle. Managing through these cycles became very difficult, and bankruptcy has been common. There have been approximately ninety bankruptcies in the industry since deregulation, including all of the major carriers. Interestingly, the two largest carriers were later acquired by smaller airlines after their bankruptcies. The merged companies wisely retained the American and United brands.

To grow and be profitable in the industry, an airline had to be the preferred carrier for some segments of the market with a cost structure equal to or lower than competitors for those same segments. Airlines have become skilled at defining segments for which their products and routes are most attractive competitively.

We put together a set of strategic options with Wolf and presented them to UAL's board. Events overtook UAL, and the board approved the takeover by the unions that year. The coalition of unions hadn't given up their dream of taking over UAL since their failed attempt with Ferris. It took six years to develop a workable plan to fund the takeover and establish an employee stock ownership plan (ESOP). The principal source of funds was a reduction in union wages and benefits below contract levels and changes to work rules. The ESOP wound up with 55 percent of UAL's common stock—majority ownership. The unions were given two seats on the board and had veto power over two board actions: sale or merger of all or a major part of the company and election of the CEO. The unions chose Jerry Greenwald, former president of Chrysler, as CEO. (You may remember from chapter one that we worked closely together for two years at Chrysler.) The airline did well during that period, becoming the world's largest airline and one of the most profitable. When Greenwald completed his five-year commitment in 1999, the board chose UAL's president, John Edwardson, to succeed him. The unions vetoed his election. The board then chose the top sales executive, Jim Goodwin, as the next CEO.

The roof fell in—with a number of serious problems. The unions went after a snap-back of their wages when the ESOP investment period ended in 2000, which was their right in their contract. UAL and US Airways (then run by Steve Wolf) agreed on a merger, but it failed when the government withdrew its support. UAL's unions also opposed the deal. Our firm was deeply involved, and I was the liaison person between the airlines. Later that year, 9/11 crushed the industry as fliers stayed home and revenues cratered. Bankruptcy was inevitable.

Glenn Tilden, former CEO of Texaco and experienced in managing through bankruptcy, was brought in as CEO a year later. UAL declared bankruptcy in December 2002 and remained there for over three years. The airline emerged from bankruptcy with a much more competitive cost structure and balance sheet. Shareholders, including the ESOP, lost almost all their investment. Four years later UAL merged with Continental, regaining their position as the largest airline in the U.S. More important, the merged airline was positioned strategically as a national carrier in the U.S., a strong international airline, and the core of the Star Alliance, which has twenty-seven members plus affiliates serving customers seamlessly across the globe.

Throughout all the drama, and continuing until my retirement early in 2002, I worked side by side with five United CEOs over twenty years. I had a cockpit seat in the turbulent airline industry, which went through bankruptcies of all the major carriers, strikes, consolidation from seven large regional carriers to three national networks, over a hundred new entrants, most of which failed, boom and bust with every economic cycle, wide swings in oil prices causing wide swings in profits, fare wars, technological changes, and massive investments as the industry asserted itself after deregulation. I learned that steering a company through those minefields drew out the best in leaders—judgment, courage, decisiveness, intellect. And to those who think the turmoil in the airline industry is over, I confidently say, "Not just yet."

The mission of the consultant (and any advisor to top management) is to understand the company and its industry from an outsider's independent and objective perspective. Your value to your client depends on your ability to see opportunities and risks for the company that others may not see and to persuade top management to act.

In the United Airlines case, there were many such incidents. A consultant never takes the credit but does have the satisfaction of seeing ideas implemented and the client prosper. United was a very satisfying relationship. Throughout those twenty years, United and American were in a dogfight for industry leadership. Both airlines had the right to claim victory several times. Both suffered major setbacks, including bankruptcy. And the battle goes on as both airlines merged with other major carriers and continue the dogfight—which now includes Delta Airlines—in one of the most competitive industries in the United States. Despite all of the problems within the industry, the number of passenger miles has quadrupled since deregulation while fares in real terms have halved, and U.S. airlines are among the safest in the world. Air is by far the safest form of transportation.

Consultants don't take credit but can take pride.

As this book is going to press, the airlines are confronted with another huge challenge—the coronavirus, which has dropped revenues by 70–90 percent throughout the world. While the outcome is unclear, the industry will again be changed, probably dramatically, but my bet is that the best run and financed companies will survive and prosper again. The world needs a strong airline industry.

AMOCO

One day I was flying to New York and by chance was seated next to Dick Morrow, the CEO of Amoco. Morrow and I had become acquainted through civic activities in Chicago. Mitzi and I went to the opera each year with Dick and his wife.

Standard Oil of Indiana was one of the companies created by the breakup of Rockefeller's Standard Oil Trust in 1911. It subsequently changed its name to Amoco, the American Oil Company. Amoco was in the top dozen integrated oil companies in the world in reserves, petroleum exploration, production, refining, and its sales and distribution network. It also had a large petrochemical business.

Our conversation drifted toward the company and a major issue with which they were wrestling. Oil prices had quadrupled in 1973 when OPEC, the cartel of Middle Eastern oil producers, embargoed deliveries to countries that supported Israel in the Arab-Israeli War. Prices drifted back down during the 1970s but spiked again in 1979 when OPEC again curtailed volume. Prices moved down sharply again during the recession of 1982. Amoco was convinced that prices would remain low for the foreseeable future. OPEC was having internal problems maintaining volume discipline as member states violated their commitments to satisfy economic needs at home. Saudi Arabia, the leader of OPEC, showed little interest in enforcing discipline.

Amoco's conclusion: Cut costs to a level that would enable a good return to shareholders at the current oil price and keep costs there. If the price of crude increased, Amoco would have a windfall. The size of the cost reduction would be large—over 20 percent across the board. Two executives, Larry Fuller and Jim Cozad, had been charged to figure out how and to get it done. We spent the rest of the flight talking about how companies have undertaken such major restructuring, including our recent experience with United. Morrow asked me to talk with Fuller and Cozad.

Larry Fuller, president, had spent his career with Amoco, run most of the operating divisions, and was the heir apparent to Morrow. Jim Cozad had joined Amoco twenty-five years earlier from Philip Morris. He was vice-chairman and chief financial officer. They set up a meeting with the top operating execs of Amoco—lunch at the Chicago Club. I arrived five minutes early, which was ten minutes late in Amoco time, a lesson I would never forget.

Time is relative and very important. Learn when it's OK to be on time, rather than early. Never be late.

We filed in to lunch in a private room. Fuller and Cozad made opening remarks, then all eyes turned to me. There was no formal presentation. I simply didn't know enough about their company or their situation. Rather, my discussion focused on what other companies had done with similar objectives; then I turned the meeting into a round-table discussion. Good decision. The discussion was robust. These were not wallflowers or unsure people. My conclusion: They were committed to the mission, but each had a different path to achieve it.

The goal was to reduce current costs to produce strong profits at the current oil price (around $40 a barrel) and maintain that cost level going forward. Historically, cost levels rose with oil prices, often much faster than inflation. The goal would be profitable operations independent of rising and falling oil prices. Since prices at that time were low, it was unlikely that prices would fall much below current levels. This assumption held true for thirty-eight years, until the coronavirus halted transportation in 2020 and oil briefly dropped to zero.

Our role was to work with the Amoco leaders and team members to develop and execute a plan to achieve permanent cost reductions without adversely impacting operations. We pulled together a small team headed by Bruce Pasternack, a relatively new partner with good oil experience. Gary Neilson, who had been a very effective manager of our United cost-reduction work, was the overall project manager. We had agreement from Fuller and Cozad that "everything was on the table."

A cost reduction of this magnitude had to include all activities in the company and would likely involve restructuring the way Amoco operated—e.g., how to manage production from the wellhead to the refinery, how to run the refineries and the huge network of service stations, how administrative services were conducted, and how resources were allocated.

We quickly found the "sacred cow"—the field production offices. Amoco justly prided itself on its management of drilling and well production. There were five levels of management from the wellhead to the president—great control, but huge costs.

My hypothesis was that three levels could get the job done without losing control; and that this would result in major cost reduction. But that would never sell unless the recommendation came from inside. We set up a team to study the production process, headed by the most respected production manager in the company. We guided the analysis, but he was involved at every step.

The VP of production, Hank Boswell, also had to be convinced. The team recommended that the field offices be eliminated. Not reorganized, *eliminated*. We scheduled a small group meeting with Boswell. This would really be a hard sell since in our initial interviews with us he waxed eloquently on the value and tradition of the field offices. The meeting went far more smoothly than I expected. Boswell agreed. The dam was broken. No one could protect their island. Tradition or history could not be used to prevent action.

Fuller and Cozad were delighted. Everyone respected and feared Boswell on his turf. To Hank's credit, he later told me that he couldn't have imagined eliminating the field offices and staffs, but the case was made and he had to put his preconceptions aside. He became an effective advocate for our work.

Facts can slay the most protected of sacred cows and convert the toughest foe.

Our joint client-consultant teams spread out to every business and major organizational unit and from top to bottom. One amusing story—the process for deciding on exploration targets went something like this: The Exploration Group proposed an investment budget based on available resources and assessment of prospects. Finance approved the investment budget for exploration based on available funds. The scientists and geologists selected places to drill based on the best technology available.

Their list was then reviewed by their managers, followed by two or three committees of the best exploration people in the company. So far, so good. Careful, objective analysis was warranted for some of the most costly and important decisions an oil company makes. Then the vice president of exploration brought these recommendations to a special committee of Amoco top executives for a final decision. Beyond the vice president of exploration, that committee had few people with exploration experience at any time in their careers. The committee had a dedicated room with a large table on which the maps were spread out and held flat by bean bags. Given the importance of the decisions to the future of the company, it was not surprising that meetings were well attended and long. The discussions were lively, and everyone gave their opinions.

It was like Sir Georg Solti discussing his approach to Bruckner's Fourth Symphony with a group of orchestra trustees and taking their counsel seriously. Only worse, Solti could not be outvoted. The tradition was clear—these were the cardinals responsible for the Holy Grail, and once elected a cardinal you took your responsibility very seriously and wouldn't consider delegating those decisions. We took the issue to Fuller and Cozad, who agreed the senior committee was unnecessary, though both said they enjoyed it. The risk with the extra committee was that the people truly responsible for the decisions might not feel the buck stopped with them.

Decisions should be made by those responsible for results. Proper delegation is critical to good decisions.

Over the next two years Amoco met its objectives. Our firm continued to work with Amoco on a variety of improvement projects for several more years until the company was acquired by British Petroleum.

Several staff professionals became partners in our firm. They created the successful Booz Allen's Oil and Chemical Practice led for years by Bruce Pasternack. Gary Neilson became a senior partner, published a book, *Results*, which captured the process and spirit of what we did at United and Amoco, and became one of the firm's most prolific client developers.

A strong relationship with top decision-makers based on mutual respect and trust is the best formula for achieving tough objectives.

Every company needs to reinvent itself periodically to maintain leadership as economic, market, and competitive conditions change.

The United and Amoco experiences confirmed what I had observed with Chrysler and several other clients. Most companies become (very) cost-inefficient over time, having added activities and management layers to address current problems, but rarely, if ever, stepping back and reassessing the best way to achieve their mission and goals. In my experience, such an assessment can reduce costs by more than 20 percent even with highly successful firms, while actually improving the company's ability to achieve its mission and most important goals.

SUCCESSION

A few years later, Jim Farley announced that he would be stepping down as CEO. The firm had a tradition of managers returning to full-time consulting at age fifty-five and retiring at age sixty. All previous CEOs had been chosen by their predecessors, which wasn't much of a tradition since there had only been three transitions in seventy years—Ed Booz to Jim Allen and then to Charlie Bowen and finally to Jim Farley. Farley decided that the board would choose his successor, which set off a competition since there was no heir apparent. The process took several months and narrowed down to about five senior partners—four from the commercial business and one from the government business. All were capable, successful professionals. The government partners strongly supported their candidate, and the commercial partners were divided among the other four. Mike McCullough, the head of the government business, emerged as the new CEO.

Clearly, this was a personal disappointment. I had looked forward to the opportunity of leading the firm and felt ready. The decision put me at a serious crossroad in my career—to stay and continue doing work that I loved, or to leave and seek an opportunity to become a CEO elsewhere. I was at the right age and level to change careers. The question lingered in my mind for several months. A few calls came inquiring about my interests, but they were never seriously followed up. Other partners who were in the running left the firm, though not for opportunities that would have been attractive to me. Subconsciously, the bar was set high because my life at Booz Allen was very satisfying professionally. As time passed, so did the urge to leave. We always wonder what could have been, but will never know. Nevertheless, the next eighteen years at the firm were highly fulfilling professionally, and I am glad I stayed the course.

Disappointment, however deeply felt, is not a justification in itself for making a major career decision. Rather, we should use disappointments to ask ourselves what is truly important. Career disappointments happen to everyone several times in a lifetime. I have been lucky to have had only a few.

BOOZ ALLEN ADVISORY BOARD

Sometimes an off-the-wall idea can lead an executive or company in directions they didn't realize were possible. One such idea in my Booz Allen career was the creation of an international advisory board.

For years the idea of an advisory board for the firm with leading CEOs from around the world was kicked around. The biggest objections were that no "leading CEO" would accept an invitation with a management consulting firm and that it would cost much more than the value we might derive from it. In the late 1980s, I raised the topic again as chair of the Operating Council. I had been leading an effort to acquire Kissinger Associates, a foreign-policy consulting firm founded by Henry Kissinger shortly after he left government in 1976. After a year of discussions and meetings, Kissinger decided that he preferred to remain independent.

Instead, he suggested creating a Booz Allen Advisory Board with "leading CEOs from around the world" and Henry Kissinger as chair. Over that year he had grown to like and respect Booz Allen and wanted to be part of it, but without losing his independence. I loved the idea and took it to Mike McCullough. He suggested taking it to the Operating Council. "If the senior partnership wants to do it, we should." Our senior partners were intrigued but concerned whether we could pull it off. Nevertheless, at the next Operating Council meeting they approved the idea with caveats and agreed to let me try.

Kissinger was delighted. Although he had been out of government for over a decade, he maintained close relationships with world leaders and respect achieved by few in history. We assembled a group that exceeded my expectations. Over its ten-year run, the advisory board had seventeen members from ten countries. Their companies were leaders in their industries. All members were leaders in civic, professional, and charitable activities. All were extraordinary individuals. Fewer than a third were previous clients with our firm.

We scheduled a meeting every nine months in cities in which we had offices. The meetings were focused on major strategic issues facing the firm, for example, entering a new country or new area of consulting, the economic and political outlook, how to improve the impact of consulting, and our long-term strategy. Discussions were robust. Bob Galvin, CEO of Motorola, would typically remain silent until called on to give his take on an issue. Invariably, he would start with, "Very interesting comments on an important topic, but . . ." Bob was one of the most insightful and effective business leaders I have ever known. One example: We were discussing the strategy of the firm over the next five years. After his windup came the *but* . . . "You should have a planning horizon of twenty or more years, time for a new generation of technology, time to consider how new staff and partners should be educated and developed, time for new economic and political systems to take root, time for you to change the management consulting profession. A five-year time frame limits your thinking to what you know today and will doom you to incrementalism." Galvin was the father of the mobile phone revolution.

We had several memorable meetings. Attendance was always high, which was amazing considering the schedules of these individuals and the travel involved. Two truly unforgettable meetings were in Paris and in Rome. The Paris meeting was set around the final game of the 1998 World Cup between France and Brazil. The night before the game we took our group of dignitaries and their spouses to the Three Tenors Concert in the shadow of the Eiffel Tower. The following day we had a motorcycle escort through the impossible traffic on the *périphérique* to and from the stadium. France exploded with pride that night in celebration of their victory. Pierre Rodocanachi, our leader in Paris, was a magician organizing that trip.

The Rome meetings included an audience with Pope John Paul II and a meeting with the prime minister. I will never forget Lita Young, wife of Lord Young, a former U.K. minister and chairman of Cable & Wireless and one of the few Jewish members of the House of Lords, hauling an armful of rosaries from the Vatican Museum to be blessed personally by the Pope for her Catholic friends back in London.

We never solicited business from our advisory board members, although several became new clients. All were excellent ambassadors for the firm. The benefits far outweighed the costs in terms of the firm's reputation, new relationships, and sound advice from otherwise unreachable sources. Importantly, the advisory board members told me how highly they valued their time with a small group of top business leaders from across the world and being exposed to the firm's intellectual capital. Several obtained counsel from our partners whom they met at meetings. I became personal friends with almost all of the board members, visiting them in their home cities and obtaining their counsel on our firm. My personal network expanded widely through them and their friends. Finally, my time with Henry Kissinger, from our first meetings to discuss merging our firms through all our travels together, which included my membership in the America China Society, which he founded and chaired, was one of the most enjoyable and rewarding relationships of my career. He is a unique treasure for our country and for the world . . . and he has a great sense of humor.

Sadly, the advisory board was disbanded when I retired in 2002. We did go out with a bang in Rome, however. I was disappointed but believe those were ten wonderful years, and the effort was rewarding for Booz Allen and all who participated.

An advisory board can give a firm access to individuals who would not be available to serve on a board of directors. Discussion can be tailored to areas of highest interest to your firm. The cost can be nominal.

ANOTHER NEW JOB

Mike McCullough asked me to head the commercial business in the U.S. It was an exciting time because we had shifted the organization from geographic offices to industry and functional practices. Partners and professional staffs were now the responsibility of practices. The executive group for the sector was populated with the heads of the most important practices—banking, manufacturing, information technology, healthcare, systems, strategy, and operations. We had some of the best professionals in their fields in that room, several of whom went on to extraordinary follow-on careers. For example, Ray Lane became the president of Oracle, general partner of Kleiner Perkins, and chair of Carnegie Mellon University. Bob Howe turned IBM Global Services into a major consulting company and subsequently became CEO of Scient, a dot-com darling of the 1990s with Howe as a cover boy on *Forbes* in April 2000. Dan Lewis later headed the firm's commercial business. The practices served clients, did research, built intellectual capital, became experts in their areas, developed staff and new partners, and built relationships in their industries globally. The fundamental mission, however, remained to serve our clients.

A jolt of new energy shot through me as we dealt with the way we served clients and how we grew professionals and the firm. Batteries recharged, I headed toward sixty with as much energy as I had at forty. Over the next two years, the firm had a resurgence of growth.

People are capable of productive work far longer than we have assumed. Forced retirement at sixty, sixty-five, or even well into the seventies can be a giant waste of any country's best assets—experienced, knowledgeable, energetic, wise professionals and executives. Surely it is the same with research scientists, authors, doctors, carpenters, plumbers, psychologists, teachers, and virtually any other professional.

We often force our master craftsmen into retirement at sixty-five in the United States. Why? The key factors for continuing productively at any age are good health and a spirit that is switched on by the satisfaction and excitement derived from the work.

As I moved into my sixties, I realized that I wanted to continue working, but that the challenges had to be fresh, so I resolved to change careers at sixty-five while I still had the stamina to take on new challenges. The idea of settling back in the "rocking chair" or playing golf five times a week sounded horrible. I sought out new boards to join, and small companies to invest in and counsel, along with making deeper dives into my not-for-profit activities. And I wrote my first book.

THE TRILLION-DOLLAR ENTERPRISE

Booz Allen became involved in the World Economic Forum (WEF) in the early 1990s. Paul Anderson opened the door with WEF Executive Chairman Klaus Schwab for the firm to be an active participant. I went to my first meeting in Davos, Switzerland, in 1991 and gave a presentation on the changing structure of international business. The *Economist* magazine liked it and gave my speech a full page in its next issue. My partners encouraged me to develop the ideas further and write a more comprehensive paper for distribution to our clients. Some thought I should write a book on alliances. I gave talks on the topic over the next several years, but didn't take writing a book seriously. My sons, Stephen and Scott, thought the concept was intriguing and warned me that the world was moving quickly in the direction I had predicted. If I didn't do the book soon, it would be history rather than foresight. The formation and success of the global airline alliances OneWorld and Star were instructive examples. So I got to work.

For the next year, research and writing occupied every spare moment, including the bulk of our vacation at the Mona Lani in Hawaii. *The Trillion-Dollar Enterprise* was completed in the spring of 1998 and published just before Christmas. The book tour included TV appearances on CNBC's *Power Lunch* and Chicago PBS station WTTW. The book was translated into five languages: Cantonese and Mandarin Chinese, Japanese, French (thanks to my partner, Pierre Rodocanachi), and German, plus there was a British edition. The experts told me that sales of 25,000 in the U.S. plus an unknown number internationally was good for a business book.

The premise of the book was that alliances had advantages over acquisitions for companies expanding internationally. Through alliances, companies would be able to serve more markets and obtain more technology with less capital and less risk than by buying another company. Alliances legally skirted protective regulations and laws in several countries. As markets and economies globalized, so had competition and supply chains. The result would be giant enterprises with global networks of alliances and extraordinary product, market, and geographic reach. Some would exceed a trillion dollars in sales or assets.

A number of industries have consolidated through alliances. Airlines and banks are prime examples, but virtually every global industry has experienced a surge in alliances. The book remains relevant for its examination of the rationale for alliances, how to determine when and where they are appropriate, and how they should be managed.

My last several years with Booz Allen were spent on clients and working with younger partners to develop clients and relationships in the community. When the time came to retire, I was ready, and I had no interest in continuing to work with the firm on a part-time basis, as many retired partners did. My "to do" list was lengthy—including writing, speaking, serving on corporate boards, reading all those books gathering dust in my library, travel with Mitzi, golf in Florida, and a significant increase in community activities. The bucket list was long. All those plans went up in smoke when Chiquita came along.

Plan for the future, but always keep an open mind to new opportunities and challenges. You never know what might show up on your doorstep.

Chapter Seven

FROM CONSULTANT TO CEO

"Yes, We Have Bananas"

In February 2002, the month before I retired, I was asked by my son Stephen, then a partner with Och Ziff hedge fund, to join the board of Chiquita Brands International, which was coming out of bankruptcy—right in my strike zone. It's a complex tale with lessons in everything from geopolitics to international law to branding to how to tell when a banana is ripe.

Chiquita was an extraordinary experience. It was my first opportunity to be a CEO after thirty-five-plus years of counseling CEOs. There is a big difference between advising and deciding. As managers, you are playing with live ammunition. Nevertheless, I took the problems and decisions just as seriously as a CEO as I did as a consultant. This made the transition relatively easy.

During my two-plus years in the CEO saddle, we were faced with virtually every type of problem—excessive cost and debt, environmental issues and pressures, huge swings in our stock price, ethical and legal challenges, selling and acquiring businesses and starting new ones, dealing with impossible investors, battling to save or expand clients and customers, strategy and improving the business model, and traveling around the world to expand our footprint. The experience drew on everything I had learned during my consulting career and all the energy, creativity, and discipline I could muster.

Och Ziff and four other hedge funds had bought Chiquita bonds at a heavy discount, which had been converted to equity in the bankruptcy. Thus, the five former bondholders held the majority of Chiquita's equity. They selected the post-bankruptcy board. Carl Lindner, the chair and largest shareholder pre-bankruptcy through his American Financial Group, and Chiquita CEO Steve Warshaw were carried over to the new board, and five new directors were added.

Chiquita had been driven into bankruptcy by a bad strategic bet. The company concluded in the early 1990s when the European Union was being formed that trade barriers would fall and that bananas from the plantations in the Caribbean and Central America would be freely traded across Europe. Chiquita had strong market shares and profitable operations in northern Europe, where bananas were imported without duties from Latin America, but weak shares and struggling operations in the U.K., France, Spain, Portugal, and Italy, which had protective trade arrangements for their banana-producing former colonies.

Chiquita bought additional banana plantations and invested in specialized refrigerated ships to transport Caribbean-grown bananas to the new EU. It would be ready to supply the new markets as soon as the treaty was signed and the protective duties were dropped. In the final EU negotiations, however, the countries that had banana-producing former colonies were allowed to continue duties on bananas imported from Latin America. The potential increased market for Chiquita disappeared. Chiquita had taken on major debt to fund its purchases of plantations and ships. It was a roll of the dice that did not pay off. Current operations were unable to service and pay down those debts. Cash reserves were depleted, and the company filed for bankruptcy in 2001. While there was great uncertainty about the EU's 1992 program, there were many voices warning in advance that lots of programs like banana imports were being keenly lobbied. Chiquita's bet might never have been made if the level of uncertainty had been known.

If you're doing business internationally, make sure you have access to information and insight from people or think tanks on the ground.

The five new board members had a series of meetings before we assumed office in March 2002, when the judge was scheduled to complete the bankruptcy proceedings. We realized we needed a new chairman. I was about to retire and had more time than my new colleagues. Consequently, they nominated me to be the non-executive chairman. Situations like that occur all the time in business.

The new board members met with CEO Warshaw in Cincinnati. Strangely, he wouldn't bring any of the other executives into the meetings, despite our requests. His principal interest appeared to be the board's committee structure. We wanted to know about the business and financial situation and his plans going forward. His answers on the financials and operations gave us serious concerns. He finally called Bob Kistinger, the head of the banana business, when we insisted. Kistinger was knowledgeable and forthcoming with information. My alarm bells were going off. The more we learned, the more we concluded that we needed to replace the CEO. At our next meeting, the new board members asked whether I would take the CEO job for up to two years.

You never know what life holds for you. Be prepared.

Chiquita had been a dominant brand in the world. The Chiquita jingle created in the 1940s was repeated on the radio millions of times.

Anyone who was alive then remembers the jingle and most can sing parts of it. "I'm Chiquita Banana and I'm here to say, you have to treat bananas in a special way . . ." For years the brand enjoyed a premium price and commanded the leading market share. Retail outlets offered several brands, and Chiquita was the leader.

In the 1950s and 1960s supermarkets in the U.S. took over mom-and-pop neighborhood grocery stores and subsequently consolidated the retail food market regionally and then nationally. The big supermarket chains had extraordinary purchasing power and used that leverage to drive down prices with their vendors. They began to bid out the banana business and carry only one brand in each store—and then in each region. The Chiquita brand was not strong enough to cause a customer to change stores if their favorite store stopped carrying it. That supermarket practice destroyed the brand value of Chiquita almost entirely in the U.S. We did find that several retail chains believed that its customers preferred the Chiquita brand and continued to carry Chiquita, but there was no price premium. Chiquita continued to be one of the top ten most recognized brands in the country.

Never confuse "brand recognition" with true "brand power."

A commodity business is managed differently from a brand business. Commodities are sold on price and service, with no expectation of a premium over competition. Virtually all bananas grown and harvested in the Western world were one genetic strain, the Cavendish. Hence, the only product differentiation came from the ability of the producer to get the banana to the market in good shape.

The top three producers, Chiquita, Dole, and Del Monte, supplied 80 percent of the market. All had the ability to deliver a quality product. Consequently, the low-cost producer wins. To the grocery chain, the all-in cost includes the purchase price of the product and other costs such as transportation, ripening, distribution, waste, and handling. Chiquita had been treating bananas as part brand and part commodity—including advertising.

We developed a strategy for Chiquita in the U.S. that treated bananas as commodities. In Europe, grocery stores continued to carry multiple brands, so we retained our brand strategy. The U.S. strategy had three major near-term objectives: (1) substantially reduce costs—we set the target at $100 million—remember, the low-cost producer wins; (2) divest non-performing assets; and (3) drive a major reduction in debt. We announced our three goals to our shareholders as a "capital C" Commitment.

We retained my former partner at Booz Allen, Jill Albrinck, to run the cost-reduction program. The board was so impressed with her that they "ordered" me to hire her. It took all of my persuasive skills to convince Jill that she should move to Cincinnati rather than New York, where she had another opportunity, but she did join and was a major contributor as a top executive.

The company had gone through serial cost reductions before and during the bankruptcy, so the easy cuts were long gone. We had to change the way we did business without adversely impacting the customer or the product. It was tough, and we had to play it straight with the employees, who had been through the hell of bankruptcy.

At a meeting with employees discussing what we were doing and why, one employee raised her hand and said, "This could mean I might lose my job. Right?" I said it was possible. We would keep as many of our best people as possible, but reducing the staff was necessary. I promised we would make the cuts professionally and work hard to help employees find new jobs elsewhere. It was on everyone's mind. I saw no way but to face it directly and be honest with everyone. And we did reduce the staff considerably and met our $100 million goal.

Next, we had to identify and divest or close non-performing businesses. After several months reviewing the performance and prospects of each of our businesses, canned vegetables stood out as our weakest.

There were three major players in canned vegetables in the U.S. It was a commodity business with virtually no differentiation in the consumer's mind among brands, only price. Ten cents on a forty-can case at wholesale could swing the order. It was a third of our company's volume and had been built up over the years through acquiring small brands. Margins were razor-thin and, including overhead support, the business was losing money.

We saw no way to reduce costs enough to make Chiquita the low-cost producer of canned vegetables. Doubling down by acquiring a competitor was out of the question. Returns were too low to invest in that business. We concluded we should sell. Fortune smiled on us. I got a call from a major competitor, Arthur Wolcott, CEO of Seneca Foods. He said one of us should sell to the other and he would like to buy our canned-vegetable business.

We agreed to have lunch in Sea Island, Georgia, on my way to Florida that weekend. I put on my best game face as he tried to convince me that selling to him was the right solution for both of us. Over the next month, we figured out a price, and the deal was done. It was, in fact, a win-win for both of us. We were able to reduce our debt by more than $200 million and stop a drain on earnings.

We analyzed each of our banana-producing properties and discovered that one of our two plantations in Panama was nicely profitable and the other was a real drag, both financially and emotionally, because of an obstreperous union. Our analysis showed that we would be better off if that plantation became a third-party supplier rather than owned by Chiquita. The key was to obtain a reliable supply of quality product at a good price. It took six months, two personal visits with the president of Panama, countless hours of negotiation with the union leader, and a few strokes of luck to conclude a deal to *give* the plantation to the union.

The union boss wanted to have total control of the equity, and we wouldn't agree. In the end, a committee of union members excluding the union leader was established as a board and the president of Panama endorsed the deal gratefully. We signed a purchase agreement to obtain the quality product we needed to serve our customers, which enabled the new owners to transition the company profitably. Another non-performing asset was gone.

Early in the process when I first met with President Mireya Moscoso, she observed: "You know, if this meeting had occurred some time ago, you would be telling me what you were going to do rather than asking for help." I knew instantly we were going to get along well. President Moscoso was instrumental in concluding the deal.

When politics are involved, businessmen need to think like politicians, too.

That led to the final item on my agenda: reducing the company's post-bankruptcy debt load. A combination of selling the canned-vegetable division, improving profitability through cost reduction, and shedding unprofitable assets enabled us to take much of the debt off the books. Delivery on three important "commitments." That year we titled our annual report *"Commit and Deliver."*

Commit and Deliver is good for everything you do in life.

During the cost-reduction efforts, we were faced with continuing the expensive environmental and social responsibility programs that had been initiated in recent years—e.g., funding adequate housing and schools for workers, continuing research on chemicals used for controlling fungus and insects, and obtaining Rainforest Alliance environmental certification for all our farms. Jeff Zalla, our head of Corporate Responsibility, made compelling arguments for retaining our commitment to the environment and social responsibility. Chiquita had come a long way in redressing mistakes it had made in previous decades. Chiquita had turned around its reputation as a corporate pariah. We explicitly exempted those programs from the cutting block.

The only time I ever appeared on a magazine cover during my career was with the CEO of Ben & Jerry's on the July/August 2003 issue of *green@work* magazine for receiving company awards for environmental excellence. Ben & Jerry's, the co-awardee, made the prize seem truly meaningful, since it was an environmental icon. Chiquita's transition was stunning. Example: I was giving a talk about Chiquita at the World Economic Forum in 2004 when a participant publicly criticized Chiquita for treating workers poorly. Before I could respond, the president of our farm workers' union interrupted to defend Chiquita as a leader in social responsibility. When visiting banana-growing sites in Central America, I always spent time on worker and environmental conditions. Workers cared deeply about those issues, and so did management.

The true corporate performance is not just about revenue and profits. In business, numbers tell a lot of the story, but never the whole story.

THE 100TH ANNIVERSARY ON THE NYSE

In February 2003, Chiquita was asked to ring the opening bell on the occasion of our 100th anniversary on the New York Stock Exchange. We, of course, accepted. Ringing the bell is not important to anyone except the company doing it.

On the day before Chiquita was to ring the opening bell, CQB (Chiquita) was the worst-performing stock on the NYSE and hit a post-bankruptcy low of $8. That news was on the wire. I learned what real depression felt like. I couldn't face the scene and the cameras the following day and called to cancel Chiquita's appearance. I asked Bob Olson, our general counsel, to inform the board and our management team. Late that night, I received a call from the youngest member of our management team, Jeff Zalla. He gave me a tough "Knute Rockne" message to stand up and ring that bell with pride. We did and I will forever be thankful to Jeff for that call. We can look back on the bell as the beginning of a great turnaround.

We had just hired a new Miss Chiquita, who joined us on the podium in full regalia on her first day on the job. I asked her how she liked her new job and she responded with a beaming smile. As she danced through the floor brokers on our way to the CQB station, no one thought about yesterday's horrible performance. Eighteen months later the stock traded at $30 per share.

Joe Pickler, CEO of Kroger and a Notre Dame alumnus, invited Mitzi and me for dinner at his home one evening, along with Rev. Michael Graham, S.J., president of Xavier University, where Joe was a trustee. It was a delightful evening discussing Xavier, Notre Dame, the Jesuits, and the rehabilitation of Cincinnati, which was a top priority for Pickler. At the end of the evening I told Joe, "I would like to work for you" (he almost choked) "for a day." I explained that I wanted to experience the point of sale of bananas from the customers' and grocers' points of view. Kroger was one of our largest customers and carried Chiquita exclusively in its Cincinnati stores. My proposal was to spend a day as a worker in the produce department in one of their stores. Only the store manager could know who I was. This occurred before the TV show *Undercover Boss*.

Two days later, I trudged across a snowy Kroger parking lot bundled in the oldest clothes I had in my closet and made my way to the produce department. No greeting committee, but the department manager had been told that an old guy needing a job was coming in. "Put him to work." A single mom in her fifties took me under her wing and explained the rules. She asked if I had brought my lunch and gave me a worried look when I said no. She warned me to keep my receipt for things bought in the store and taken to the employee lunchroom. She took me around the department and explained my job. She also began to tell me her life story and the problems she was having with her sixteen-year-old daughter. Fortunately, she didn't ask me about my life so I didn't have to fabricate. She took me to the lunchroom and went about her job for most of the day, checking in regularly. She was a good soul.

The experience was excellent. In the morning, the bananas were displayed perfectly—clean, orderly, full bin, sorted by color from green to bright yellow, sprayed lightly with water. The customers went right for the middle color, yellow with green stems, and worked toward full yellow as the bin emptied. I went to the produce manager and asked if we could refill the half-empty bin. Unfortunately, there were no more bananas in the storeroom. I suggested that we call the distributer for more yellow and was told that another delivery was coming in the afternoon, and they were to be yellow. A shipment of green bananas arrived in the afternoon. No one else realized, or cared, that lots of sales were lost because almost no one bought green bananas, even when they were all that was left. Pickler and our distributor got copies of my report to our logistics department. Conclusion: a day well spent.

Understanding your customers at all levels is important in every business and experiencing your customers' activities firsthand is priceless.

OTHER POTENTIAL MARKETS

Early in my time with Chiquita, we took a world tour of our operations and markets. Asia was an untapped market for Chiquita, so we visited Japan (our principal market in Asia), the Philippines (our source of bananas in Asia), and China (a country that loved bananas), where we ripened our bananas in someone's basement. In fact, China, India, and Russia consumed more bananas than the whole rest of the world. Why not Chiquita's?

We needed a good source of bananas near China. The plantation in the Philippines was on the southern island of Mindanao, which was in the middle of a civil war between the country's Muslim and Christian factions. On my first day with Chiquita, *The Wall Street Journal* published a front-page article describing the bizarre situation in Mindanao in which the war was suspended during the day while workers from both sides harvested bananas together on Chiquita's plantation. On my visit to the Philippines, they treated me like a head of state—armored cars, high speeds through villages, armed guards everywhere. This was not a place where we should invest and expand.

In China, we visited the new breadbasket for the country in the southern province of Hainan. The Chinese were very interested in Chiquita investing there. They were building a new port and could easily supply Japan and the eastern cities of China from that location. Unfortunately, the climate wasn't suitable for year-round growing. Banana plants drop seeds that grow into new plants, a process enabling year-round harvests without new planting. Replanting every year would kill cost competitiveness. We crossed off the Philippines and southern China as sources of increased production. Later I contacted Ratan Tata, CEO of Tata Industries and a former member of the Booz Allen advisory board, about a joint venture in bananas in India. He suggested we meet with the head of Tata's food and agribusinesses. Regrettably, nothing developed. An opportunity for another day.

On another trip, to Russia, Bob Kistinger and I met with a major Russian food distributor in St. Petersburg. He was clearly interested in carrying Chiquita and treated us very well. Something was "off," however. There were too many bodyguards in the compound of warehouses and offices, and his questions led us to believe that security was a major issue. We had been forewarned that the local mafias and security were big problems in food distribution. Kistinger and I concluded that Chiquita wasn't ready for Russia despite the potential size of the market.

There is no excuse for trying to do international business without knowing the players and the countries intimately. Most failures are caused by lack of one or the other.

Sometimes the best deal is the one left undone.

We took the Chiquita board to Costa Rica to witness growing, harvesting, and shipping bananas. The board resisted the idea of flying to Central America for a meeting, but were happy they did because they got a firsthand view of the challenges of delivering a banana to a customer's kitchen in perfect condition for such a low price. One of the highlights was the Banana Olympics, which pitted teams and individuals in each step of the picking, sorting, and packaging process. Fun and exciting.

A board should have firsthand knowledge of the products, services, and customers of the company it serves. As a consultant, a director, and a CEO, I have encouraged management and boards to get to the plant, the stores, the customers. I share that belief with you and hope you encourage your boards to do the same.

TO SELL OR NOT TO SELL

Almost from the day I became CEO, certain shareholders, including former bondholders, had let me know that they believed that it was in the shareholders' interest to sell the company. I learned that the former bondholders agreed among themselves that their exit strategy was to sell the company as soon as possible. In fact, they had meetings with potential buyers during the bankruptcy. In my former life as a consultant, I didn't have to listen to shareholders. That was the responsibility of management and the board. But it was now my job, and I discovered it was a big part of that job.

Always understand the interests of your stakeholders. The board is hired by its stakeholders and must consider their interests when making decisions.

There were two logical buyers. One was Fyffes, a large Dublin-based food distributor that handled Chiquita's business in Ireland, the U.K., and a few other countries. The other was Dole, the second-largest banana producer.

David McCann, CEO of Fyffes, visited us in Cincinnati shortly after we took over the board. We discussed expanding our working relationship and a potential merger. Fyffes was a private company, owned principally by the McCann family. He wanted to merge with Chiquita in an all-stock transaction, become the majority shareholder, and take over management of the combined enterprise. Fyffes would become a public company through the reverse merger. Although it was smaller and less profitable than Chiquita, Fyffes put a higher valuation on their business. It wasn't clear how this would be an attractive exit for the ex-bondholders. His position was a non-starter, but we agreed to keep the door open.

On my first trip to Europe for Chiquita, Bob Kistinger and I met with the whole family, including Neil McCann, the father, patriarch, and principal shareholder of Fyffes. It was clear that they were still interested. I learned much more about their business and genuinely liked and respected the family, but their position on ownership of the merged companies hadn't changed, although they attempted to dress it up more attractively. We left the door open for further discussions, which never took place on my watch.

I called David Murdock, CEO and principal shareholder of Dole. Our bondholders had met with him during the bankruptcy so I knew he was interested in Chiquita. Murdock invited me to visit Dole's headquarters and have lunch with him at his home in Thousand Oaks,

California. Bob Fisher, one of our directors who became executive vice president of Chiquita when I became CEO, was the former president of Dole. Fisher briefed me on Dole and on Murdock.

We met first in his office, where Murdock told me about the history and current situation of Dole, with cameo appearances from several of his executives. It was clear that King David was in charge. Murdock was in his late seventies, but appeared to have the fitness, energy, and mental agility of a man in his forties. He was proud of what he had accomplished, and particularly proud that he did it with an eighth-grade education. He noted that Carl Lindner had one more year of school than he did. Murdock was a master strategist and, underneath a smooth gracious manner, was tough as nails.

We went to his home for lunch, where we were joined by his son, David Jr. The home itself was comfortable, but more modest than I expected. The grounds, however, were suitable for a seventeenth-century European monarch. Twenty-ton monolithic rocks, which he had shipped from the Mekong Delta in Vietnam, lined a magnificent mile-long *allée* between his house and a cluster of buildings, including a research lab for vegetables and fruit. Along the *allée* was an outdoor amphitheater for private concerts with the likes of the Los Angeles Philharmonic. Grazing on the other side was a herd of black sheep, I think Murdock's favorite animal.

We discussed his interest in Chiquita, which was clearly high. I couldn't understand why he was interested. Dole was very successful; he had more wealth than he could possibly have imagined. He had just personally acquired huge real estate holdings, including Lanai Island in Hawaii; and he said he planned to buy the outstanding shares of Dole and take the company private. His biggest challenge appeared to be succession. His children were not interested in running the business.

Why add Chiquita on top of that heap, particularly in light of an almost certain challenge by the Department of Justice? He told me a story. When he was very young, his family was poor. One of his school friends had a nice big house and an electric red train in his basement playroom. He had always wanted an electric red train. Chiquita was his red train.

Chiquita stock went back on the market post-bankruptcy at $14 per share. Shares had traded between $8 and $18 and were around $16 at the time of my visit. Murdock suggested a price of $16. When I left, I told him that we could be interested, but not unless the offer started with a "2". We talked a few times after that, but he never put another bid on the table.

POSTSCRIPT

Chiquita bottomed at $8 in 2003 and peaked around $30 shortly after I retired in 2004. A decade later, Fyffes made a run at Chiquita but was beaten out by Brazilian buyers—Cutrale Group, Brazil's largest orange juice producer, and the investment firm Safra Group—with a bid of $14.50 per share. Most of the original bondholders had sold their stock on the open market well before I left Chiquita.

When I retired from Chiquita in 2004, I was given a cartoon as a souvenir that still hangs in my exercise room. It shows me on a ship with Miss Chiquita and flags of our strategic objectives. The ship is the U.S.S. *Commit and Deliver.*

Apply your experience and values to any role you assume and you've got a real chance to succeed.

Running a public company is exciting, challenging, frustrating, and demanding of every morsel of your skills, creativity, energy, and patience. It can also be one of the most satisfying professional experiences you can have.

Chapter Eight

CATCH A
FALLING SUN

"The World Is Made of
Stories, Not Atoms"

C hicago still has two major print newspapers and you can still buy
a copy of the *Sun-Times* on the newsstands in Chicago or have a
copy delivered to your door or your computer. It could have been
much different.

After a couple of years of retirement, I was invited to join the board
of Hollinger International, a holding company that owned the *Chicago
Sun-Times* and close to 100 community newspapers in the Chicago area.
Later I became CEO of the Sun-Times Media Group and publisher of
the *Chicago Sun-Times*.

There are a lot of lessons from that experience and from the tra-
vails of the newspaper and media industry itself. The following is by no
means a comprehensive dissection of media, but the lessons are important and applicable elsewhere.

THE NEWSPAPER

Throughout the life of our nation, newspapers have played a central role in public life. From the invention of the printing press by Gutenberg in 1440 until the invention of radio, television, and the internet, newspapers were the only form of mass communication. As a result, they gained tremendous power. Newspapers decided which events to report and what to say about them. They supported certain causes and candidates and opposed others, countered only by other newspapers or orators on soapboxes in the town square.

Newspapers were paramount in moving public opinion in every war and every election in U.S. history until recently. They have been the source of documents for historians, recording both personal and public events. Even court opinions often relied on newspaper accounts of crimes and significant events. The invention of the telegraph and the telephone enabled newspapers to be even more powerful by extending their news-gathering reach and timeliness.

But the next three major technological innovations in communications—radio, TV, and the internet—took bites out of the newspaper's dominance. Beginning in the early 1900s, Americans could listen to the voices of their leaders, and for the first time, news was broadcast instantly across geographies by radio. Newspapers' monopoly was broken, but not seriously. Despite the competition, newspapers enjoyed golden years of growth, profitability, and influence throughout the twentieth century. Even though radio could provide immediacy and actual voices, newspapers continued to provide analysis and opinions and a greater range of coverage. Hunger for timely information grew exponentially as the U.S. entered the Second World War; reporters spanned the globe to help readers learn what was happening. Those of us around at the time remember watching the newsreels *From the Front* in the local cinema before the movie started.

Television arrived shortly after the war and put far more pressure on newspapers than radio had. As Americans settled around their TV sets to watch the evening news, the demand for afternoon newspapers fell off the cliff. (Thankfully, it didn't happen when I was delivering the *Chicago Herald-American* after school in our neighborhood.) Afternoon newspapers began disappearing, one after another. It is sobering to remember that Chicago has seen dozens of newspapers begin, thrive, and die. But despite the disappearance of afternoon dailies, newspaper revenues continued to rise and readership grew on the back of a growing economy through the latter half of the twentieth century. The quality of American journalism improved dramatically, even as celebrity news, entertainment, and gossip became standard fare in the paper.

THE BEGINNING OF THE END FOR NEWSPAPERS

The internet proved to be too much for newspapers, replacing their mission rather than competing with them. It has taken thirty years since its creation for the internet to achieve almost universal acceptance, but the dam had broken. By the early 2000s anyone could obtain virtually any information important to them on the internet immediately, rather than waiting to see the morning paper. The newspaper was no longer the major "source of news."

The internet was becoming an integral force in virtually every aspect of modern life—jobs, hobbies, social networking, real estate, the economy, investments, education, sports, and politics. And we are only on the cusp of this revolution. News can be distributed to everyone everywhere at almost no cost over the internet—without the need to destroy trees and haul logs to environmentally crushing paper-making plants, to operate environmentally dirty printing plants, to send out trucks early in the morning for deliveries in snow, rain, and sleet, or to employ large distribution staffs in expensive office buildings . . . not to mention the disposal problems of old newspapers. The fall of newspapers at the hands of the internet is an excellent example of disintermediation of an industry by technology. Technology has given us a better, faster, cheaper, less environmentally invasive way to distribute information than newspapers, or any other non-digital means for that matter.

The fall of the newspaper industry will displace millions of workers in the U.S. alone, and multiples more worldwide. That's what happens when an important industry is disrupted by technology. Another good example: The horse was the primary mode of transportation for centuries until the steam engine (railroads) and the car displaced the horse. *The New York Times* published two pictures of the same street in Manhattan one decade apart. The first picture (taken in 1900) was subtitled "Find the car." The second picture (taken in 1910) was subtitled "Find the horse."

There is an argument that the cost of the decline of the newspaper to society is greater than we can fathom. Newspapers, for better or worse, have been a trusted filter. In the newsroom, professional journalists are governed by an accepted code of conduct and professionalism and supervised by editors who lose their jobs if information is incorrect or misleading. Teams of investigative journalists were organized and funded by the newspaper to provide a check on lawmakers, to uncover corruption and malfeasance, and to present opposing policy arguments. The term "Fourth Estate," meaning a strong, independent societal and political force, defined the role of the media in the democratic structure of checks and balances. Newspapers have been America's trusted Fourth Estate, at least for the past century. The internet has no accepted code of conduct or editorial review. It is the Wild West, where anyone can say anything, and there is no sheriff. In fact, one of the biggest attractions of the internet is the absence of controls. The battle between freedom of speech and society's best interests is already raging.

In recent years we have already seen a change in the newspaper's role as a "trusted source of information." The number of journalists in the newsroom has halved since 2005; investigative reporting units have all but disappeared. As newspapers fight for share of their declining markets, many have followed the example of cable news networks, slanting their coverage and interpretation of events to cater to the ideology of their target markets. Like our political structure, the media has been separating along the same fault line between liberal and conservative—so much for being "trusted and objective." Interestingly, newspapers were aligned with political parties and ideologies early in our country's history, but straightened up by the Civil War.

A democratic society needs a trusted, independent Fourth Estate. For the sake of our democracy, it must evolve on the internet.

THE SITUATION IN 2006

Readership surveys painted a grim outlook for newspapers when I joined the Hollinger board in 2006. While 75 percent of the sixty-and-older age group read a newspaper daily, only 10 percent of the twenty-to-thirty age group did. Projections for younger cohorts were for fewer readers. I fear that my grandchildren will encounter newspapers only in historical research projects. Children today become addicted to the iPad before they can read.

Advertisers saw these trends and began reducing the percentage of their total spending on print publications. Newspapers' share of total advertising dollars had dropped from its historic level of around one-third in 2005 to 16 percent in 2009, and the downward slide is continuing to 6 percent in 2021. Classified ads accounted for around 25 percent of ad revenues pre-2005. Pages were filled with small ads—a cheap way for small businesses and individuals to sell or buy anything from pets and old furniture to homes and cars. Classified ads accounted for over one-third of profits for newspapers historically. Costs to collect and print classifieds were very low; consequently, revenues went almost straight to the bottom line. In corporate-speak, the margins on classified ads were extremely high. Unfortunately, when classifieds vanished during a five-year period with the avalanche of online services like Craigslist and eBay, profits also vanished. Newspapers have not been able to capture enough of the digital market to come close to covering those losses. In fact, industry-wide from 2005 to 2009, print advertising declined by $24 billion while digital ad revenues increased by a mere $1 billion. What a horrible trade.

Amazingly, investors didn't see the fall coming. Valuations remained high through the mid-2000s. Print advertising peaked for the industry in 2005 at just under $50 billion. Valuations also peaked. In 2007, News Corp. bought *The Wall Street Journal* for $5 billion, and Sam Zell bought the Tribune Company for $8 billion. Since then both print advertising and market valuations have collapsed.

Market forces are powerful, and resources available for newspapers will continue to decline. There will be fewer and smaller newspapers with less investigative content, weaker editing, and more shared content—except for a few brands with large followings like *The Wall Street Journal* and the few newspapers that become successful in the digital world (so far none). Local newspapers with monopolies in small towns have a chance of surviving because their activities are not covered by national digital media. One study counted 135 daily newspapers in the U.S. that have gone out of business from 2005 to 2010—plus an additional fifteen that switched from print to digital distribution.

HOLLINGER INTERNATIONAL

My involvement with the *Chicago Sun-Times* came indirectly through Conrad Black.

Black is a Canadian born in 1944 to a wealthy family in Montreal. He built a privately held media empire consisting of more than

100 newspapers in towns and cities sprinkled across Canada, including the august *National Post*. Eventually, he also owned the *Chicago Sun-Times* and 100 suburban newspapers around Chicago, the *Daily Telegraph* of London, and the *Jerusalem Post*. He controlled Hollinger International, at one time the world's third-largest English-language newspaper empire.

Black was a true global media mogul. He palled around with the glitterati of Europe and North America. He called Margaret Thatcher, the prime minister of the United Kingdom, a close friend. Few doors were closed to him. He is still entitled to be called the Right Honourable Lord Black of Crossharbour. He is a respected historian, having published several well-regarded books.

To understand what happened at the *Sun-Times* it is necessary to understand how Black constructed his empire. Bear with me here: It's complicated. Black owned a personal holding company in Montreal, Ravelston Corporation, which controlled businesses set up by his father and the Canadian newspapers that Conrad had acquired. He set up a Canadian subsidiary of Ravelston, Hollinger Inc., and transferred the ownership of his newspapers to it. He then sold 80 percent of Hollinger Inc. to Canadian investors but retained supermajority voting rights with his minority stake. Hollinger Inc. subsequently set up Hollinger International as a U.S. subsidiary and transferred the ownership of the papers into that company. Hollinger International was then taken public on the New York Stock Exchange with super voting rights for the Hollinger Inc. stockholders.

Essentially, Black sold his newspaper empire twice but still retained control with his tiered holding company and super-voting-rights structure. Clever, huh? He appointed the boards of both Hollinger Inc. and Hollinger International. Black then set up a service company in Canada, owned by Ravelston, to handle administrative activities, such as legal and accounting, for the U.S. company for which it received fees. He personally received finder's fees for acquisitions and divestitures by

Hollinger International. These activities and opulent corporate spending by Hollinger International resulted in a revolution among Hollinger shareholders culminating in his ouster.

In 2004, Black was forced out by the board of Hollinger International, a result of the findings and recommendations made by a special committee of the board that shareholders had required him to appoint to investigate the company's activities. The board and certain shareholders, aided by Richard Breeden, former head of the Securities and Exchange Commission, pursued prosecution against Black for fraud, alleging he had improperly taken $92 million from the company. Ultimately a U.S. court in 2007 convicted Black of fraud and obstruction of justice. Some of the charges were later dropped on appeal to the Supreme Court. His original sentence of six and a half years in prison was reduced to forty-two months. He was released from prison in Florida in May 2013. In 2018, Black published *Donald J. Trump: A President Like No Other*, a flattering biography. President Trump pardoned Black in 2019.

I became involved in 2006. After Black was forced to resign, the board began replacing Black's original appointees. The process took a few years. My name was thrown into the hat. The turnaround at Chiquita and my long relationship with Chicago were important to the search committee. Since its holdings were Chicago papers, it was reasonable to have at least one local director. Before accepting the board's invitation, I researched whether the company's legal problems were limited to its former top executives and whether the company could survive.

I spoke with a number of the retiring directors, the members of the special committee investigating Black's dealings, and some of the remaining top managers. I met with the lead partners of the company's audit, legal, and PR firms and with several shareholders. I approached Hollinger International as I would an important new client. Eventually, I concluded that the legal risks for the company beyond Black and some of his top managers were not substantial.

Joining a board is a serious decision. Give it the same due diligence as you would joining a company as an executive.

But legal issues were the least of the problems the board faced. Hollinger's business risks were considerable. Survival was far from certain. There were two big questions to that puzzle: First, was the industry downturn cyclical or a permanent trend? And second, how bad were the company-specific problems of Hollinger International? The answer to the first question was not clear at that time, though the signs were ominous. The rise of digital communications was a serious threat to newspapers in both circulation and advertising. To the second question, Hollinger had almost $200 million in cash from recent divestitures but over $1 billion in potential tax liabilities in Canada and the U.S. Cash flow from operations was positive but declining, and the need for investments was high because the operations had been starved for years. Again, the signs were ominous. I was seventy years old and had to weigh whether I was up for the challenge of being an active board member, ready to give my time and energies to a company in serious trouble. I finally concluded that I could make a difference. Mitzi observed that I couldn't resist helping a maiden in distress.

THE SUN-TIMES MEDIA GROUP

My first few board meetings were eye-opening, devoted almost exclusively to the board's special committee investigating Conrad Black. Almost no time was spent on the escalating operating problems and risks with the industry in decline—and not a moment on potential opportunities to turn things around. I was appointed chair of the Compensation Committee. My fellow board members were less than delighted when I suggested our pay be cut.

I bought some stock, as I always did when becoming a director of a company, even though it would be a risky investment this time. We changed the name of the company from Hollinger International to Sun-Times Media Group (STMG), signaling a complete break with the Black era. The focus of the board remained an indictment of Conrad Black and his top associates, directed by the special committee.

The CEO, Gordon Paris, was living in New York and did not want to move to Chicago, so we began a search for a new chief executive. Raymond Seitz, chairman of the board and former U.S. ambassador to Great Britain, suggested I think about throwing my hat in the ring.

In the meantime, an off-site strategy meeting was organized with the board and top management. It didn't go well. The management's presentations were riddled with holes. It was clear the top managers did not understand the perilous position of the company and had no realistic plans for turning the company around. After a long, arduous day, Seitz and I agreed that the company was in even worse shape than we had thought, and its current management was not up to the task of handling the declining situation. I spent that night preparing a discussion for the board the following morning to define the problems as I saw them and a framework for a turnaround plan. After the discussion, the board scheduled a meeting for the following month to select a new CEO. A search firm was already working on it.

A number of board members contacted me to ask that I take the job; but I believed seventy-one was too old. At the November 2007 meeting, one of the directors came in whistling the theme song to the movie *Rocky*. I said, "Yeah. Rocky 10!" At the end of the meeting, I agreed to take over as CEO for up to two years.

Age is just a number. But make sure you think you can do something well before agreeing to jump in.

The next two-plus years were a wild ride—intense. It was like skiing down a steep trail of ice along the edge of a 1,000-foot cliff. My first task was to assemble a team to arrest the decline in cash flow while keeping up journalistic standards. Circulation and advertising revenues were declining rapidly. It was essential to slow or reverse the revenue decline, because it would be fatal to cut expenses for more than a short time. Five members of the new executive team were new to the company, three were promoted, and two were retained in their current jobs. It was a good team that could work well together.

Legal matters involving Black and his associates were handled by the special committee along with Richard Breeden and a team of lawyers. Breeden & Associates had been retained by the special committee. My time was devoted to operations and survival. I was worried that the legal and indemnification costs were sky high and was warned by my friend Elmer Johnson, head of Kirkland & Ellis, that even if we could turn the company around, it might become insolvent because of the huge legal fees. We asked the court in the state of Delaware, where Hollinger International had established its domicile, for relief from paying the mounting legal fees for Conrad Black—and received a resounding "No . . . Indemnification means indemnification!" Eventually we paid out more than $100 million in legal fees, one of the largest items of expenditures for the entire company. STMG settled with Black's associate and president of Hollinger International, David Radler, for $64 million. We should have pushed harder for a settlement with Black, which would have been better for him and the company.

Potential tax liabilities were life-threatening to the Sun-Times Media Group. Canada charged that Black had created an illegal organizational structure to avoid taxes and claimed the company owed $600 million in taxes and penalties. We got the sum reduced to $40 million through a favorable court ruling in Canada, but an American torpedo was still headed directly at our engine room. The U.S. government claimed the company's tax liability was between $500 million and $600 million and growing with interest and penalties. The IRS offered to settle part of our liability for $125 million. With nearly $200 million in cash (prior to the Canadian settlement), a few of the board members urged me to take the deal. To me, cash was our lifeline and without it we would be insolvent. There were no banks or creditors who would lend us money, and we had asked many. We hired a former IRS commissioner as a consultant, who suggested a number of ways to negotiate a settlement. We never came close enough together to make a deal with the IRS.

My son Stephen, who has been in the investment world since he graduated from Yale, marveled, "How can a company with $400 million in revenue, only moderate and declining cash flow, and over a billion dollars in potential tax liabilities survive?"

The Great Recession of 2008–2009, triggered by Lehman's failure, hit the print media industry, which went into free-fall. Circulation, both locally in Chicago and nationwide, was declining at more than 5 percent a year. Nationally, print advertising declined 15 percent that year, which followed a 10 percent decline the previous year and appeared to be accelerating. The *Sun-Times* papers were gaining market share, which only meant that our competitors were falling faster than we were. Tribune Company, owner of the venerable *Chicago Tribune*, filed for bankruptcy. Several other urban newspaper companies around the country were either in bankruptcy or on the brink.

The major driver of the decline was not the financial collapse of 2008, although that was dragging the whole economy down. The real cause was the shift of readers and advertisers from print to digital media. That shift by readers had been slowly escalating for more than a decade, and almost nobody in the print industry had come up with viable solutions. Our one bright spot initially had been holding on to advertisers who continued to favor print despite declining readership. We knew that could not last. And by 2007, advertisers were backing out. When asked by an investor at our quarterly earnings call shortly after I took over whether the downward trends were cyclical or permanent, I answered honestly that I didn't know. He expected my answer would be "cyclical," which was the common view. By 2010, it was clear that the trend was irreversible.

Supporting the news operation was a top priority. I considered the newsroom an important trust, the core of the company. We invested in new technology despite our bottom line. Our investigative reporting team was extraordinary even in those tough times. They had put the spotlight on Governor Rod Blagojevich and lit the fire under Mayor Richard M. Daley. In fact, the investigative team won the Pulitzer Prize in 2010. (The Pulitzer Prize was a beacon of honest, fact-based reporting, and several of its trophies graced our offices.)

Our sports reporting, a bedrock of local newspapers, was the best in Chicago. Our movie critic, Roger Ebert, was the dean of national movie criticism, although he was very ill. Our columnists, such as Carol Marin, Michael Sneed, Terry Savage, and Mary Mitchell, were creative and energetic and syndicated across the country. Neil Steinberg was a superb writer even though I rarely agreed with him. John White, our Pulitzer Prize–winning photographic journalist, was among the top ten in the country. Our editor-in-chief, Michael Cooke, performed magic every day. There should be a movie about him. My hours spent in the newsroom and lunches with journalists were treasured.

Get the consumer-facing product and services right. Then fix the business side.

As for the business side, we developed five strategic priorities. First, stabilize revenues. Can any business survive revenue declines of 10 to 15 percent a year? Advertising accounted for 75 percent of revenues, circulation 25 percent. We focused on advertising. Second, we restructured the cost base of the Sun-Times Media Group, which meant fundamentally rethinking the company's operations. I led by taking one-third the cash compensation of my predecessor. Third, protect the quality of the newspapers, that is, journalism. If we cut the quality, we would kill the franchise. (Surprisingly, many newspapers slashed the newsroom first.) Fourth, resolve the disputes we had with Canadian and U.S. tax authorities. Fifth, create and implement a digital strategy to win more readers in the digital marketplace and do it profitably.

All hands threw themselves into implementing these five priorities. We had an agreed-upon strategy and a plan. We changed the leadership of advertising, marketing, and sales twice—and our approach continually. Everyone was drafted for sales calls—including the CEO.

We turned over every rock searching for cost reductions. We outsourced the call center. We outsourced the distribution of most newspapers to the *Chicago Tribune*, long considered our mortal enemy. I met with Sam Zell, CEO of the *Tribune*, to set up a joint venture for printing both companies' newspapers and combining information technology. A printing deal was implemented shortly after I left. Although the IT venture proved a bridge too far, we increased our investment in digitalization of products, marketing, and distribution. We even outsourced the print setup for advertising to India, considered profoundly radical—but they were able to demonstrate that quality was good, and the cost effectiveness made it worthwhile. Reporters were equipped with cameras. The executive team agreed to take 10 percent of their compensation in stock. I agreed to take 50 percent. We turned the company upside down as we searched for better, less-costly ways to create and deliver the paper and deal with our customers. Survival was at stake.

Cost reduction should start at the top, which demonstrates to employees and investors that you are serious.

But nothing was enough to offset the market forces driving down revenues. We gained market share; it didn't matter. Each major cost reduction pushed our cash flow up, but one or two quarters of declining revenues wiped out the gains. It was frustrating and heartbreaking. In the summer of 2008, it hit us hard that our options were limited. It was becoming clear that there would be no return to the good old times for advertising revenues. The best we could do was slow the decline.

We were unlikely to win a tax settlement with the IRS. Large cost-reduction opportunities had been exhausted. We had to begin cuts in the newsroom. Finally, we began an earnest search for a buyer. The timing could not have been worse.

Sometimes market forces are too strong to resist. Adapt.

We began serious discussions in the fall of 2008 with Jim Tyree, CEO of Mesirow Financial, a large Chicago-based financial services company. Tyree was the perfect new owner. He was born, raised, and educated in Chicago, a native totally dedicated to his city. He was involved in a number of local organizations that focused on making life better for everyone in his hometown. He shared my passionate belief that Chicago should have two viable newspapers to give the city the competition and diversity of opinion that make a society strong. He was not going to flip the company to make a quick buck, unlike the hedge funds that had been interested.

At the same time we were talking to Tyree, three of our largest shareholders, including Hollinger Inc., initiated a proxy fight to replace the current board with a new slate of directors selected by them. Since they controlled over half of the voting shares—including Hollinger Inc.'s super voting rights—there was little doubt they would succeed. I tried to meet with their representatives to discuss the implications, but they were not interested in talking. At my last meeting with the board, I urged them to conclude a deal with Jim Tyree.

In the end, there was no solution to the U.S. tax problem. We never gave up trying to get a deal but began to realize the only way to save the newspapers was to put the holding company, Sun-Times Media Group, into bankruptcy and sell the newspapers as operating businesses—a Section 363 sale.

After the conclusion of the proxy vote, their nominees took over and I resigned. A few months later the board concluded the sale of all the newspaper properties and other assets to Jim Tyree and a group of like-minded, public-spirited Chicagoans.

Tragically, Jim Tyree died a year later. Subsequently the papers were sold to another Chicagoan, Michael Ferro. Ferro was a successful entrepreneur who believed that he could make the *Chicago Sun-Times* successful again. Shortly after buying the *Sun-Times*, Ferro become a large investor in the newspaper half of the Tribune company, briefly named "tronc." He subsequently became chairman of tronc and divested his personal stock in the *Sun-Times*. Tronc attempted to acquire the *Sun-Times* with the agreement that the *Sun-Times* would continue to be published and the newsrooms would remain independent. A group of unions and individual investors beat out tronc in an auction set up by the Justice Department. The *Sun-Times* remains independent . . . for now.

I smile when I pass the newsstand with the *Chicago Sun-Times* displayed prominently, and I read the paper regularly, pleased that many of my favorite journalists are still there.

In life you will encounter challenges that have low economic payout but great benefits for society. I hope you will take the bait.

Chapter Nine

LIFE IN THE BOARDROOM

The board of directors holds an exalted and crucial role in the capitalist system. Corporations are independent entities—limited by laws and regulations set by government—but boards, which have responsibility for corporations, don't report to anyone in a hierarchical sense. The board is elected by and "reports" to its shareholders. The board has extraordinary power and independence. The board represents the shareholders in selecting and overseeing the management and direction of the company. Some, including me, consider boards a linchpin of the capitalist system.

From the beginning of my consulting career, appearances before corporate boards were common. It was necessary to understand the role they played within their companies, the issues they faced, and the regulations governing them. My board experiences are included here to describe what goes on in the boardroom, what is required of directors, and how people become members of boards. Over my career, I served on fifteen corporate boards and over twenty not-for-profit boards.

When Booz Allen was returning to private ownership by the partners, Jim Farley asked me to lead the effort to design a new governance process for the firm. Subsequently I served on the Booz Allen board for several years. The Kellogg Governance Conference, which I helped Don Perkins and Dean Don Jacobs establish, gave me live perspectives about how directors thought about their responsibilities and the tough issues they faced. I had become a student of corporate governance, a counselor to corporations on how to establish and run an effective board, and an author of several articles on governance.

My interest in serving on outside commercial boards had two serious obstacles: (1) conflicts of interest with Booz Allen clients, and (2) resistance from management to having a consultant on the board. Booz Allen permitted partners to serve on outside boards if they did not conflict with the partner's or the firm's activities. Few ever did. The biggest exception was Jim Allen, who served on several boards. Most companies, however, did not want a consultant inside the boardroom. As John Richman, CEO of Kraft, put it to me, "You are well qualified and have great, diverse experience, but you are a *consultant*."

Several of my board experiences are described here to give you an inside view of what goes on in the boardroom—that is, what directors are faced with and how we responded.

STARTING SMALL

My first invitation to an outside commercial board came from Don Perkins and Bill Sanders to join the board of LaSalle Real Estate Fund, an investment fund for institutions. Our job was to set the value of the assets owned by the fund, which determined the price at which investors bought or sold shares in the fund. Not exactly a corporate board, but it broke the ice, and other invitations followed. The next few invitations were also from CEOs who knew me well. Don Clark, CEO of Household International, asked me to join the board of Elger Industries, a manufacturer of plumbing fixtures, which was spinning off from House-hold. Subsequently Clark asked me to join the Household International Board, my first major public corporate board.

HOUSEHOLD INTERNATIONAL/HSBC USA

Household International grew out of a consumer finance company, HFC, founded in 1878 to serve common working people. HFC was restructured a century later in 1981 as a holding company with credit cards, mortgage, and consumer-finance businesses. Household International (HI) acquired several manufacturing companies during the conglomerate craze in the 1980s. I joined the board in the early 1990s. The board was constituted principally of CEOs of large companies. Don Clark, HI's chairman and CEO, ran a tight ship and grew the company into a major financial institution in the U.S., principally by controlling costs, serving customers well, taking limited risks, adding extensions to current businesses, and excellent blocking and tackling. Clark also refocused the company on its core finance businesses by spinning off the manufacturing businesses acquired by his predecessor.

As Clark approached retirement, the board appointed Ed Hoffman, HI's president, as his successor. Hoffman died suddenly and Clark delayed his retirement until another successor could be found. In today's world it is great to have one successor in-house, but it is rare to have two ready to go. The search took almost a year. Bill Aldinger was hired from Wells Fargo in 1994. HI continued to grow by entering new segments of consumer finance such as auto loans. In 1998, HI acquired its largest competitor, Beneficial Finance, and became the domestic leader in consumer finance. The credit card business grew to become the sixth largest in the country. Aldinger's strategy was more aggressive than Clark's and aimed at significant growth in shareholder value. HI stock rose handsomely.

Aldinger believed that HI's growth was limited without owning or becoming a bank. He began to explore merger possibilities with a number of banks and bank holding companies. We came very close to a merger with Wells Fargo, Aldinger's former home. In retrospect, we should have accepted their offer. Wells Fargo appeared to be an excellent strategic fit, and the price was good.

Shortly after, HI became a target of activists who claimed that HI and a number of other subprime lenders used predatory practices in their mortgage and credit card businesses. There was a political movement in the country in the late 1990s to increase home ownership among lower-income families—spreading the American dream. Congress had passed legislation and the government pushed for lower standards for subprime mortgage loans. ACORN, a leading activist group, took their protests to our directors. One day, my assistant, Vicki Anderson, called me out of a client meeting to tell me that a large group from ACORN had taken over the lobby of our office and demanded to meet with me. They said they would stay until I returned. Vicki told me to find something else to do that day. Another director had his house picketed and "TPed" (draped in toilet paper). From my point of view, the movement to assure everyone had the opportunity to own a home was a wonderful ideal, but forcing financial institutions to change their lending practices to achieve this societal goal was insane.

HI and others who served the subprime market understood the risks and built business models to accommodate them. The political pressure on the company was enormous. HI was sued by attorneys general of forty-six states. In my view, HI's lending practices were not predatory or discriminatory; they were sensible, based on the historical risks HI learned over its century of serving people the banks would not serve. HI reached a settlement with the state governments in 2002 for $486 million and restated earnings for nine previous years. The alternative was a constant barrage of attacks from government regulators and interest groups, which likely would have driven HI out of business. This was a classic example of coercion by the government to achieve its political goal. Shortly after, HI was acquired by Hong-Kong Shanghai Bank

(HSBC), a large bank holding company in London, culminating the search for a merger partner.

Several of the HI directors were appointed to serve with HSBC Finance Company, the new U.S. subsidiary of HSBC. I became the lead director. The company and its management remained intact, but the road ahead was rocky. Pressure from Congress and the state attorneys general on subprime lenders to loosen their lending practices on their customers caused a squeeze on margins and an increase in mortgage defaults and repossessions. Fannie Mae and Freddie Mac, government-related guarantors of mortgages, loosened their standards at the behest of Congress. At the same time, packages of mortgages, which included chunks—sometimes large chunks—of subprime loans were being securitized and sold to investors, often with AAA ratings from the rating agencies.

Bill Aldinger retired, and Bobby Mehta, who had been leading the credit card business, was elected CEO of HSBC USA. Mehta was an exceptionally bright former partner with the Boston Consulting Group. He had little idea of the tsunami that was about to hit.

At an audit committee meeting in 2005, the chair of our committee, Bob Herdman, who was a retired vice-chair of Ernst & Young, asked for a clarification of "stated income," which the company used in describing its mortgage approval process. A hush came over the room, which included the CEO and top executives of HSBC, as the company explained that the mortgage applicant's statement of income was not backed up with proof of employment or source of that income. That was an "Oh-#&@%" moment. It meant that mortgages were granted to some borrowers who had little or no ability to repay the loans. How many?? How deep was the hole? In addition, many of the loans were near 100 percent of the purchase price of the property.

A few months later HSBC took a $2 billion-plus write-down of their U.S. mortgage portfolio, the largest write-down in the bank's 140-year history. HSBC was the first major financial institution to take such a write-down, but certainly not the last nor the largest. An avalanche of subprime write-downs by financial institutions, and the failure and subsequent bailout of Fannie Mae and Freddie Mac, along with the failure of Lehman Brothers, triggered the financial crisis that brought the global economy to the brink. It is not misleading to say that the subprime mortgage problem was the match igniting the financial meltdown of 2008 and 2009. Many experts believe it was the root cause.

I retired from the HSBC-USA board two years later. We had recovered financially, but HSBC top management subsequently concluded that acquiring Household International was not the best strategy for HSBC to enter the U.S. market. They began dismantling the company, which was completed by 2016.

When you become a member of the board of directors of a public company, be prepared to spend whatever time is necessary when trouble knocks on its door.

The best of companies experience difficult times, and problems can come from many, often unpredictable directions. Don't be defensive; just deal with it.

SECURITY CAPITAL GROUP

Bill Sanders, the former CEO of LaSalle Partners, asked me to join his board at Security Capital Group, a real estate investment firm he was starting up. The invitation followed an unusual "interview" by Sanders. Bill and his wife, Cita, invited Mitzi and me for a weekend at their ranch in New Mexico. Sanders had bought what seemed like half the land between Albuquerque and Santa Fe for his ranch and planned a beautiful hacienda. In the meantime, they had a small prefab unit in the middle of the ranch. Each morning we left at sunrise to herd the cattle into another sector for feeding. Neither Mitzi nor I had been on a horse since grammar school. Mitzi rode Hollywood and I was given The Widow Maker.

The experience was a perfect introduction to a very successful run led by the most creative CEO I have worked with. Sanders had dinner alone with the outside directors before each board meeting, a practice I adopted as a CEO. Sanders would describe a new business he was considering, a potential acquisition, a new incentive program, a few recent key hires, or countless other bold moves he planned for the company. No charts. No special books of data. Just a fireside chat with his partners. The board was Fortune 100 quality—all CEOs like Sam Bodman, Larry Fuller, and Jack Frazee—so they were able to build on Sanders's ideas and give him valuable counsel. At the board meetings, Sanders trooped out his managers and new employees, who were universally outstanding. He built a team unmatched in the real estate world. Virtually every new business he launched succeeded; most were home runs. The firm grew rapidly and profitably, completed a successful IPO, and eventually was acquired by GE Capital for $4 billion. Several of the businesses created by Security Capital have become major independent firms in their sectors.

Having the right CEO makes work on the board easy, fun, and rewarding.

It was clear to me that the principal way I was going to be invited to join boards would be personal relationships. In fact, my participation on all but one of the fifteen corporate boards on which I served was initiated by a person on the board who knew me well. The one exception was Hollinger International, which had a search firm to find new directors. I met their specs for a Chicagoan with CEO and troubled-company experience. Even then, an exiting Hollinger director, Henry Kissinger, who knew me well, promoted my candidacy.

If you want to serve on boards, develop a network of executives who are CEOs and board members.

The regulations and expectations of directors of public companies changed considerably after passage of Sarbanes-Oxley in 2002. Independence became more tightly defined and enforced; director responsibility and liability grew teeth; and time commitments for directors at least doubled. Current CEOs, the most sought-after people as directors, were limited to one or two outside boards by their own boards. On the flip side, director compensation escalated substantially. Consequently, both the corporate boards and individuals interested in joining boards took greater care in making their selections. I invested considerable time in deciding whether to join each board, but did make one mistake.

MICROAGE

MicroAge, based outside Phoenix, was a Fortune 500 supplier of computing equipment to corporate and institutional clients. The market was strong and swept all participants upward. Within about eighteen months of my joining the board, results turned south. While most of the businesses were doing well, it became apparent that MicroAge's largest business—over half the company's revenue—was sub-scale in its market segment, unprofitable, and deteriorating, and it could bring down the company. MicroAge had to either acquire to achieve competitive scale or sell its core business. Since the company didn't have the resources to acquire and desperately needed the cash a sale could generate, sale was the answer. The target list was short. The CEO agreed, sort of, but didn't follow through aggressively. The company's financial condition deteriorated further. I took the unusual step of calling an executive session with the outside board members to discuss my concerns through a report that demonstrated why we were in danger of bankruptcy.

The board quickly split into two camps—two directors saw the problem as I did and the other three believed the CEO could pull the company out. That camp of three had been through a previous bankruptcy at MicroAge, which the company survived. My conclusion: If you had been through the "Long March" with a leader, you would probably follow him off a cliff out of loyalty. They were clearly loyalists. I was looking for a solution to the company's urgent problem without firing the CEO and suggested a compromise—to appoint a chairman either from the current board or from the outside who would take control of the sale of the weak business and help the CEO run the other businesses. By that time we had identified the right purchaser who, I knew, was interested. We were at a stalemate, and a vote would have supported the CEO because he would be the tiebreaker. I should have resigned . . . but didn't. A false sense of loyalty to MicroAge made me think that I shouldn't leave a sinking ship, but stay to get the best outcome for the shareholders.

MicroAge did go bankrupt and was liquidated.

If a company is going in a direction that is not in shareholder interests or if it pursues policies counter to your values and you cannot change that course, you must resign from the board of directors.

Fortunately, I had no other situations as serious as that at MicroAge, but was emboldened to express my concerns aggressively.

ALLEGHENY ENERGY

Paul Evanson, an acquaintance from our village in Florida, had been recruited away from president of FP&L, Florida's largest electric utility, to become CEO of Allegheny Energy, a struggling electric utility based outside Pittsburgh. Allegheny had followed the path of diversification into trading and financial services, which several other utilities such as Enron of Houston had led in the 1980s. Managements focused on high-margin and high-risk businesses rather than operating their utilities most efficiently and effectively. Allegheny Energy was bordering on bankruptcy and the stock sank to $3 per share. In the first six months, Evanson replaced most of the management team, got out of the non-utility businesses, and recruited a new board. He asked me to join because of my experience with Chiquita and turnarounds as a consultant.

During the next five years, Evanson focused intensely on upgrading operations, introducing several new programs to improve quality and customer service, reducing costs, upgrading and expanding facilities, and building the management team. The results were spectacular, and the stock price reflected the improvements. Allegheny became a textbook case of how to turn around a failing company and how to run a first-rate electric utility. The board meetings were active, with few disagreements on the aggressive moves the management took to make Allegheny become best in class in power generation, distribution, and customer service. The board visited plants, distribution centers, customers, and political leaders in the regions we served.

One issue loomed large. Most of its power generation (about 80 percent) was coal fueled. Allegheny had invested heavily in scrubbers and other technologies to reduce harmful emissions. It was fully compliant with current environmental regulations. It became clear, however, that the future of coal in generating electricity would be under increasing attack as environmental regulations tightened and coal became a political lightning rod. Carbon-free coal-burning generators were a long way off, even though the technology was proven in the lab. Switching to nuclear was off the table because new regulations made nuclear prohibitively expensive, and the environmental lobby had virtually killed any new nuclear plants. It was always a mystery to me that the environmentalists were at the forefront of attacking nuclear-generated energy, rather than supporting research for safe nukes. Nuclear is one of the only alternative energy sources with the scale to replace hydrocarbon generation. Allegheny explored all other sources of energy and concluded that the cost to convert from coal was beyond the company's financial resources and would be far too risky.

We decided to seek a merger partner with a balanced portfolio of generators with less coal that could manage such a transformation. The primary criteria were complementary businesses and large potential synergies that could result in a significant premium. Allegheny was an attractive merger candidate because of the regions it served, the condition of its facilities, and the quality of its operations and management. It was also quite profitable. We would have liked to be the acquirer because we believed we had the best management team in the industry, but realized that was probably unrealistic. It took about a year to find the right partner. First Energy of Ohio acquired Allegheny in February 2011 for about $28 per share, eight years after Evanson took over a failing $3-per-share company. It was an excellent fit for both companies. Evanson agreed to stay on as vice-chair of First Energy for three years. I told him that he wouldn't stay for six months, and I was correct. He is now a part-owner of the Pittsburgh Steelers, the Pittsburgh Penguins, and the Miami Marlins, and happily retired in Florida.

My experience was superb. Working with Evanson and the other board members was a pleasure. He listened, was never defensive, and was decisive. I rotated among the board committees, chairing the Compensation Committee and serving as lead director for the final year.

It is hard to overstate the importance of having the right CEO.

VIRGIN AMERICA

In 2005, Cyrus Capital decided to make a major investment in a start-up U.S. airline sponsored by Sir Richard Branson, CEO of the Virgin Group of the U.K. Virgin was owner of two airlines, Virgin Atlantic in the U.K. and Virgin Blue in Australia, and a host of other businesses under the Virgin brand. Because of U.S. regulations, foreign ownership could not exceed 25 percent of the voting stock and 50 percent of the economic value of a U.S. airline. Branson found two U.S. hedge funds, Cyrus Capital and Black Canyon, to partner in their venture. My son Stephen was aware of my twenty years of consulting with airlines and asked me to serve on the board of directors. They put together a terrific board—Don Carty, former CEO of American Airlines, as chairman and Sam Skinner, former Secretary of Transportation, as vice-chair, plus a strong and outspoken supporting cast. One special note: I had the opportunity for the first time to work with Stephen as fellow board members. Priceless.

My first board meeting was in July 2006. Fred Reid, then CEO, and I had dinner together the night before the meeting. Fred spent the bulk of the evening telling me that the company was out of cash and he was planning to announce bankruptcy the following Tuesday unless he received significant funds immediately. My well-scripted questions about strategy became irrelevant. When the initial funding was provided to Virgin America in 2005, the consensus among those involved was that the certification process—the approval to fly in the U.S.—would take three to six months, as was customary with past start-up airlines. With that assumption tucked in their minds, the company ordered airplanes and began building an organization, with the expectation that revenues were just around the corner. But they underestimated the resistance and influence of the legacy carriers, which fought ferociously to derail Virgin's application, extending the process to more than two years.

In retrospect, the industry's reaction was predictable: Why should they allow a start-up, low-cost carrier with a well-recognized and positively viewed brand to waltz in and take their market share? At least not without a fight. As the approval process dragged on, the legacy carriers believed that if they delayed the process long enough, Virgin America's backers would throw in the towel rather than invest more than their models showed would be profitable. This was a very reasonable strategy on their part, and it created the dilemma that I saw when I arrived. What the legacy carriers didn't understand was the commitment that Branson was willing to make to establish the Virgin brand in a high-profile way in the United States. Branson saw Virgin America as his entry into the U.S. for all his businesses. Every time there was a potential crisis, funds were found. This scenario was repeated several times over the next nine years, always ending in a miraculous rescue from one source or another.

Virgin America began flying on August 8, 2007, a glorious date etched in airline history, at least from our perspective. Certification took two years of *Perils of Pauline*–style, nail-biting cliff-hangers and a spectacular performance by an extraordinary management-board-investor partnership. The last-ditch act of the Department of Transportation was to demand that we replace our CEO, Fred Reid, with someone "more American." Reid was born, raised, and educated in the U.S. with U.S.-born parents and had been president of Delta Airlines. His sin was that he was selected by Richard Branson, a U.K. citizen and principal investor. The logic was that Virgin America had to be free of excess influence by foreign owners. Reid's most important contribution was to replicate the spirit and enthusiasm of the Virgin brand that Branson had created within his Virgin companies. That spirit was the soul of Virgin America.

Our new CEO, David Cush from American Airlines, didn't miss a beat and built a great organization, and Virgin America became the fastest-growing airline in the U.S. for the following decade. We had plenty of challenges. Oil prices doubled from about $70 per barrel when we started flying to over $140 in 2008, dropped to $60 for a short time in 2009, and fluctuated between $90 and $110 most of 2012 and 2013. Fuel was 25 to 40 percent of the cost structure, depending on the price. Other costs were relatively stable, rising with volume. When oil prices are low, airlines are very profitable. Above $130, the whole industry teeters on bankruptcy. Oil prices fell in 2014, and crashed in 2015 and 2016, driving down our costs.

It took eight years for Virgin America to become profitable, primarily because of high oil prices that dominated its early years. Nevertheless, the airline grew from six planes at the start to sixty-three in 2016, when it was acquired by Alaska Air Group, the parent of Alaska Airlines.

Virgin America had become one of the most decorated airlines, with nine consecutive "Best Customer Service" awards by Condé Nast and industry-wide recognition for superior customer satisfaction. The tag line, "Make flying fun again," was a reality. Customers actually fell in love with the airline. Operations were professionally run. For years Virgin America was the leader in on-time service. Virgin America pioneered a new level of in-flight entertainment with its seat-back consoles providing movies, TV, and internet. One of the best parts of board meetings were the rollouts of the latest customer-pleasing ideas—such as communicating with other passengers by phone, ordering meals from your seat at your convenience, a rock-and-roll safety video, delightful ad campaigns, updates to the state-of-the-art website, super-healthy passenger meals that we tested at board meetings, new seating configurations, and the next generation of in-flight entertainment. The route network linked the East and West Coast cities and began to link the West Coast with middle America, including Dallas, Chicago, Denver, and New Orleans.

Virgin America had a successful IPO on November 13, 2014, closing at $30 per share, 30 percent over the targeted opening price. Stephen and I rang the opening bell at the NASDAQ that day. Our airline performed well during the following year, with strong growth in revenue and earnings. Nevertheless, Stephen recognized the limits of our growth as an independent carrier and raised the issue with the board. I agreed that the timing was right, maybe even perfect, to consider a merger. We decided to have exploratory discussions with a few airlines. These quickly morphed into a bidding war between JetBlue and Alaska, with Delta ready to jump in. Prior to the first bid, the price had settled around $30. On May 6, 2016, we signed a merger agreement with Alaska Group for $57 a share.

The board, management, and Virgin team were sad to sell the carrier, which had become much more a cause than an employer to them, but they were pleased that the new owner was an airline with the same commitment to and success in customer service. The combined airline is still much smaller than the giant legacy carriers, but big enough and good enough to cater to a large customer base with excellent service. My term as a director concluded with the closing of the merger in December 2016, which marked the first month since I graduated from Notre Dame, fifty-nine years earlier, that I wouldn't receive a paycheck. I was officially, really retired. To soften that blow, the board members have lifetime passes on Alaska Airlines.

Two of the most important decisions in investing are:
1. **what and when to buy and**
2. **when to sell.**

Cyrus Capital got it right on Virgin America. In addition, Cyrus Capital participated in several of the financial rescues during Virgin America's exciting life as an independent enterprise. The timing was even more fortuitous in view of the coronavirus pandemic, which has recently grounded most planes across the world.

Corporate boards proved to be enriching professionally and enjoyable personally. All fifteen boards on which I served were unique experiences. There is no doubt that I grew my understanding of how businesses worked and how to deal with tough, even corporate-life-threatening situations from a very different perspective than a consultant's. Nine of the corporations were publicly traded companies; five were acquired; two had IPOs; two filed for bankruptcy; three were start-ups; six were turnarounds; five had changes in the CEO. Two chose me to be the new CEO, and all had major challenges.

Board membership was not a normal career path for a consultant or any professional service provider to corporations, e.g., lawyers, investment bankers, public accountants, brokers, etc. Most independent directors are current or former CEOs and senior executives in related fields, with a sprinkling of academics and service professionals. Today, the largest pool of new directors come from underrepresented classes like women and minorities.

Remember that virtually all boards are on the lookout for strong new members. If you are interested in serving on corporate boards, here are a few guidelines to consider:

- Create a network of people who are on boards and let them know of your interest. Seek their counsel. A good mentor is priceless.
- Conduct serious, objective due diligence to ensure the company meets your standards and you meet their needs. Know the company before you interview for the seat.
- Bring something of value to the table that the firm needs.
- Learn what makes a good director, how to behave in a boardroom, and how governance should work. Understand the regulations and rules.

Here are some additional thoughts on performing as a director of a corporation:

- Do your homework for every meeting of the board and its committees. Understand the company, its strategy, its businesses, its people, its industries, and its challenges. Think like a CEO.
- Get to know the top executives and other directors, not as chums but as professional colleagues. Treat them with respect.
- Add value with every comment you make in every meeting. Build a reputation for adding value; people will pay more attention to what you say.
- Be courageous. When necessary, disagree. Put company interests before your own.

NOT-FOR-PROFITS BOARDS—
SERVING THE COMMUNITY

If you learn anything from this book, it should be this one:

Serving society is everyone's duty, and the obligation grows exponentially with your success. No matter how down and out you are or how rich and successful you are, giving back and contributing your talent, material goods, and time to the good of society or the guy in the line next to you is essential to your self-esteem . . . and the future of our society.

The obvious way people give back to society is through donations to worthy causes—from small to very large, depending on your income and wealth. In my view, personal involvement is even more important. Contributing time and special skills to make your community better is a gift that only you can give. And the impact you have and the satisfaction you earn can be incalculable.

Upon our return to Chicago from Europe and New York, I immersed myself in the community. Jim Allen and Don Perkins were my primary mentors. Jim Allen was a strong believer in community service—good for the community and good for business. His advice: "Select a few organizations whose mission you believe in and devote enough time to have an impact." Allen introduced me to Perkins, whom he had mentored for years in business and community activities. For the next thirty-five years, Don Perkins was a mentor and close friend, guiding me to become involved successfully in the community.

CIVIC COMMITTEE

My first involvement had a major impact on my city and on me. Shortly after I met Perkins, he called me with my first project. The economic and social situation in Chicago was declining seriously. Manufacturing employment, the city's backbone, had dropped steadily for a quarter of a century. The K-12 public school system had been declared the worst in the nation by President Reagan's Secretary of Education. City tax revenues were in decline. Racial conflict was widespread, even on the City Council. The media dubbed it the "Council Wars." The city's business climate was worsening rapidly, with many long-established businesses leaving and few moving in. Chicago was on its way to becoming a Rust Belt casualty. Perkins, who was putting together a small team to define the problem and develop options to turn Chicago around, invited me to join.

The next six months were fascinating—an in-depth introduction to aspects of my native city I had only cursorily thought about. Silas Keene, president of the Federal Reserve Bank of Chicago, put his research department to work documenting every statistic relevant to the city's economic past and future. The numbers painted a clear and dire picture of decline, with no clear path to a reinvigorated future. Booz Allen and Arthur Andersen offered their consulting skills to study the plight of several comparable cities and actions those cities were contemplating or implementing. We pondered: Where would new jobs come from? What would happen to displaced workers whose skills didn't fit the requirements of growing industries? How does a city that relied on heavy manufacturing—dubbed Rust Belt—revitalize itself?

With the stark facts before us, we shifted our focus to figuring out solutions to transform Chicago to a stronger economic future. We started with the premise that transformation would be painful for many, but that great opportunities were in front of us. We concluded that the decline in manufacturing was not reversible, but that Chicago could become a world-class center for finance, trade, entertainment, professional services, and technology. We understood that the private sector was key and had to take the lead. We found that the cities that were successful in remaking themselves possessed one major thing in common—CEOs of companies headquartered locally locked arms to help and were personally involved.

The Commercial Club of Chicago had been in existence for one hundred years and included just the leaders we needed—in business, the professions, and education. The Commercial Club was famous for sponsoring the Burnham Plan of 1909, which had transformed Chicago into a beautiful, functional, modern city on lovely Lake Michigan. After its stellar achievement with the Burnham Plan, however, the Commercial Club devolved into a lunch-and-dinner social organization. It had to be awakened to action. Perkins got the president of the Commercial Club, Karl Bays, to establish a Civic Committee and sent invitations to sixty CEOs of Chicago's largest companies. The acceptance rate was a soul-pleasing 100 percent, even though each was asked for a commitment of $100,000 per year and a pledge of no substitutes at meetings—the CEO was the member and had to attend the meetings and become personally involved in committee efforts. Don Perkins deserves the credit. His invitation was impossible to turn down. I was asked to be a founding member—with a commitment to provide services rather than cash.

Meetings were well-attended, although a busier group of people would be hard to find. When help was needed, members provided staff, or made calls to politicians. The Civic Committee set up a consulting group to help local government institutions improve their operations. The teams were staffed by employees of member companies and led by professionals at local consulting companies. The Civic Committee worked hand-in-glove with city leaders to improve the local economy, bring in international trade, and improve education, transportation, and infrastructure. An important side effect was to mold a cohesive leadership group of Chicago CEOs. In all my travels to every part of the world, I have never seen a more closely knit group of business leaders than in Chicago at that time. And I learned, again, an old but valuable lesson: If you want action, go to the person in charge.

A number of subcommittees were set up to accomplish specific goals. For example, Elmer Johnson, a prominent lawyer, undertook the effort to reconfigure the city's roadways and public transportation networks and to fix the impending gridlock and knit the metropolis together for the next several decades. Committees were set up to tackle the failing public school system and the expansion of O'Hare International Airport, which are discussed in the next two sections as examples of how the Civic Committee operated.

The private sector is a powerful force for identifying and implementing change . . . and the best way to harness that power is to enlist its CEOs to lead.

CHICAGO PUBLIC SCHOOLS

My first major project for the Civic Committee involved the K-12 Chicago Public Schools (CPS), which were in abysmal shape. Physically, school buildings were deteriorating. Finances were bankrupt. Classrooms were overcrowded and unsafe. Test results were among the poorest in the nation. Teachers were discouraged, and morale was rock bottom. Strikes were annual events. Most important, the children who needed a good education the most to climb out of poverty and despair were the victims.

Educators had studied the situation endlessly and had long lists of the reasons for the decline of the schools, but no effective solutions. The U.S. Department of Education had spent billions of dollars but had produced almost nothing to show for all the money, time, effort, and political promises. As chairman of the Civic Committee's Education Committee, I knew we would not find a silver bullet to solve the problems of Chicago's rundown schools. So we focused on clearing the obstacles to progress—the school system's budget, how schools were governed, union activity, parental involvement, and physical impediments to a good education. The attitude of the public, the politicians, parents, teachers, and students had to be changed from hopelessness to expectation of a better future. We worked with the city council, the school board, the mayor and governor, the Illinois legislators, parents and students, and the teachers' union.

The budget was a mess, with some fifty pots of money designated for specific purposes. Management had little control over how money was allocated because federal, state, and local lawmakers micromanaged school district budgets legislatively. My favorite example: Funds were allotted every year to inform children about the patron saint of Poland, St. Stanislaus, because Chicago has a large Polish population and someone back in time didn't want children to forget the patron saint of the old country. If the money wasn't spent on St. Stanislaus, it was taken away. No matter how arcane the cause, the pots of money were inviolable.

Ultimately, the Illinois legislature agreed to reduce the fifty pots to a few, giving the schools' management flexibility to put money where they believed it would produce the best results for children. Federally sourced funds remained in a dedicated pot. The educators would have accountability for educating.

The school board consisted of seventeen elected representatives from seventeen districts in Chicago. We attended several school board meetings and interviewed school board members. In their view, the representative's mission was to get money and jobs for their district. I went to an education summit, which should have been about how best to educate the neediest children in Chicago. Ha! The main topic was teacher employment and supplier contracts—passionate arguments about subjects totally off point for an education summit. The school superintendent was in an impossible position. Superintendents were appointed by and reported to the board, which had over a dozen conflicting views on what should be done, most heavily self-serving. The current system of electing school board members was counterproductive.

Our committee concluded that the mission and focus of the school board had to be changed to target the education and welfare of children.

Stunningly obvious! The school board technically reported to the State of Illinois, but in fact no one at the state level took responsibility for the board. And who would want to take responsibility for such miserable results? It was necessary to place authority and responsibility for the education of Chicago's children in the hands of a city-wide elected official. To do the job, that official had to be able to appoint the board and the management of the Chicago Public Schools, have control over the budget . . . and be responsible for results. The obvious person was the mayor of Chicago.

We persuaded Chicago mayor Richard Daley, Illinois governor Jim Edgar, and the state legislature to agree that the mayor would appoint the board, rather than districts electing their own representatives. Thus, the mayor, elected by all the voters of Chicago, would control the board and the budget and own responsibility for the school system. Of course, this was highly controversial. If you didn't like the mayor, you didn't like the plan. If you had a stake in the status quo (and how the money was spent), you didn't like the plan.

To his credit, Rich Daley realized that if the schools continued to decline as they had been, the city itself was in increasing trouble with the declining quality of the workforce. He said repeatedly that after public safety, education had to be Chicago's highest priority. A new board was appointed. A new superintendent was put in place. Local boards were created at the school level with parents, teachers, and caring local citizens. The CPS organization was restructured to downsize the central staffs dramatically and establish district superintendents to bring management closer to the schools. The teachers' union agreed with all the changes and pledged not to strike for at least five years in return for a five-year contract.

Costs came tumbling down. Investment in facilities rose. Children cannot learn properly sitting in broken desks with plaster falling down on them and failed heating systems in Chicago's winters. New emphasis was put on educational standards and test results. The local school boards became advocates for improving their schools; a number of principals lost their jobs. Articles began appearing in national publications about Chicago's turnaround, but I warned not to engage in victory laps. There was still a long way to go. I didn't know how prescient that was.

The grinding reality of poverty, the intransigence of criminal behavior, the pervasiveness of drugs and gangs, and the worsening instability of families have prevented the true renaissance we all hoped would happen. While the improvements made in the 1990s were real and resulted in a better educational environment, conditions in Chicago's inner-city poor neighborhoods have worsened. Armed gangs rule several of the toughest neighborhoods, where the murder rates are beyond comprehension.

So much more needs to be done. In my view, the biggest opportunity for a quantum improvement is to give parents a choice in where their children go to school, a voucher system. Chicago's parochial and charter schools educate about one-eighth of Chicago's inner-city children. Given the state of the inner-city public schools and despite past improvements, I am convinced that the best path for a child to get through high school, go to college, and become a productive citizen is for that child to attend a charter or parochial school. This does not mean abandoning the public-school system, which will always educate the majority of the city's children.

There is little debate about the advantage of charter and parochial schools in lower drop-out rates, higher test scores, the percentage going to and being graduated from four-year colleges . . . and physical safety. The statistics I have seen are overwhelmingly in favor of the charter and parochial schools.

One additional advantage that is rarely mentioned is the discipline and moral values gained from a parochial (Catholic) education. There is no argument that the average child in a poor neighborhood who goes through parochial or charter schools does better in life than his or her counterpart from the same neighborhood in a public school . . . not to mention that they will have less probability of being killed or sent to prison. Unions fight to prevent school choice, arguing that money spent on charter or parochial schools will be taken from the public schools and inevitably they will decline even more. I counter, first, that we have a duty to each child to give them the best education we possibly can; and, second, public schools will improve or perish if they must compete with better-performing parochial and charter schools. The good public schools, and there are many, have no problem competing. CPS will maintain or even increase their per-student funding levels because the cost of vouchers to non-public schools is lower than the funding per student in the public system. Hence, vouchers mean more money per student in the public schools without a tax increase.

Thomas Sowell, one of the great economists of our time, makes an overwhelming case for the value of charter schools in his well-researched and documented new (2020) book *Charter Schools and Their Enemies*.

Education of those at the lower end of the economic scale is one of the most important issues facing the next generation. Get involved.

O'HARE AIRPORT EXPANSION

The Civic Committee concluded that Chicago O'Hare International Airport, which had been a major factor in the growth and development of Chicago as a hub for transportation, trade, business, conventions, and tourism in the 1950s, 1960s, and 1970s, was falling behind. Opened in 1957, O'Hare had become the busiest airport in the nation. After its first three decades, O'Hare had become overcrowded and logged the worst delays in the country, a nightmare for travelers. The Civic Committee believed that expanding O'Hare was vital to the city's future. Continuation of the status quo would result in an economic hit to Chicago, which would be unacceptable for every sector of the community. A committee was formed of Chicago business leaders.

Expanding O'Hare provoked some of the fiercest public debates I have ever witnessed. Local communities around the airport were convinced more planes and a larger airport would doom their neighborhoods. More noise, greater traffic congestion, and risks to public safety would be intolerable to them.

As a member of the O'Hare Committee, I was asked to conduct a study to determine what should be done. We fielded a team of consultants and volunteers to understand the current situation, study delay data and costs, determine the impact of an increasingly dysfunctional airport on the city's economy and reputation, and evaluate the cost/benefit of expanding O'Hare. The case for expansion of O'Hare was strong—in my mind overwhelming. The numbers were so compelling that all but the coalition of communities directly surrounding O'Hare quickly saw the benefits of an expanded airport to the city of Chicago and its neighbors. Our next hurdle was to convince the major airlines that expansion was in their interests and worth the significant share of the costs the airlines would have to pay.

While we were lining up the airlines to support the expansion, the committed opposition grew in strength and power. For three years the battle over expanding O'Hare raged in the press, the legislature, the courts, and local neighborhoods. A special tax was levied by the councils of the towns surrounding the airport to support the lawyers leading the fight against the expansion. The opposition came up with a proposal for a third Chicago airport located in Peotone, a small agricultural community seventy miles south of Chicago. Another proposal was made to expand the small airport in Gary, Indiana, to become a third airport for Chicago. Our firm analyzed both proposals. We examined the experience of cities around the world that built second airports to provide capacity that original in-town airports couldn't supply. Again, we concluded that expansion of O'Hare was the best answer.

Frank Considine, a savvy political strategist, was chair of the O'Hare Committee. Considine was chairman of the board of American National Can and served on several major civic and educational boards in Chicago. Expanding the airport threw the Civic Committee right in the middle of a complicated political battle. Under Considine, the committee decided to push for expansion of O'Hare. Considine was followed as chair of the committee by Lester Crown, the leader of one of the country's most successful business families, with a long tradition of community service. Crown used all of his skills to win government approval of the expansion. Leaders like Considine and Crown get little recognition for their enormous contributions to our city. Instead, they are compensated by extraordinary respect and admiration of their peers.

Of course, implementation was delayed, again and again. At one point, an old burial ground was discovered under land needed for the new runway. There were endless environmental obstacles, and the court cases against expansion piled on. Although the process was far more arduous and contentious than the Civic Committee expected, its members continued to put their collective muscle behind projects that benefitted the city of Chicago, despite the political and media hassles. The first phase of O'Hare's expansion was completed in 2005. The second new runway is under construction and scheduled to be completed this year, thirty years after the Civic Committee launched its O'Hare Committee. The benefits of expansion to the city have been extraordinary, exactly as our study forecast. Getting things done through the political system can take longer and be harder than you can imagine.

Only undertake community projects you are committed to and have the patience and endurance to see through. The opponents believe you will give up if they make it long enough and tough enough.

STATE OF ILLINOIS FINANCES

Illinois had been increasing its pension liabilities for decades. Pension and health benefits were easier to grant to unions than wage increases because they didn't impact the current budget as directly. It had reached a point at which the state couldn't afford to keep the pensions funded. The result was ballooning unfunded pension liabilities.

The Civic Committee set up a committee headed by Jim Farrell, former CEO of Illinois Tool Works Inc. The first report was scathing. Pension liabilities were bankrupting both the state of Illinois and the city of Chicago. The Chicago public school system was also heading for bankruptcy. The solution was clear. Pension rules and benefits had to be reduced, and action should be taken now because the solution would have to be more radical with each coming year. Illinois had passed California as the state in the worst financial condition in the nation.

The *Chicago Sun-Times* published the results and recommendations. (I was CEO and publisher at the time and a member of the Civic Committee.) It took five years and several more reports from the Civic Committee for the politicians and the public to understand the gravity of the situation and take action. The Illinois State Supreme Court then ruled that no changes could be made to government pension benefits for active or retired employees without a change in the state's constitution. Checkmate. Illinois already was among the highest business- and personal-taxed states in the country. High taxes were already driving companies and wealthy individuals out of the state, so tax increases were not an attractive option. Bond ratings for Illinois and Chicago continued to decline and hovered just above junk levels. Illinois' bond ratings were the worst in the nation. Hence, further debt would be expensive. The exodus of taxpayers from Illinois led the nation. The gridlock in Springfield prevented any political solution.

This story will play out over the years to come. The solution is unclear, but something has to be done. The private sector must participate. Sitting on the sidelines and complaining about the dreadful politicians accomplishes nothing. Whether seeking out and supporting individuals with the capabilities, values, and commitment to make a difference as elected officials or becoming involved directly as the Civic Committee has, the private sector must accept its responsibility to have good government. Never throw in the towel.

You don't have to be a politician to make a great difference in politics.

CULTURAL, SOCIAL, HEALTH, AND EDUCATION ORGANIZATIONS

There are almost unlimited opportunities to serve your local community. You should choose areas and ways of serving that match your unique interests and abilities. Examples from my experience show the breadth and variety of potential activities and the types of things you may consider doing.

My wife and I enjoy classical music, so we volunteered with the Chicago Symphony Orchestra (CSO). Mitzi served as the president of the Women's Association, which held fundraising and educational programs in the community, and became president of the Association of Major Symphony Orchestra Volunteers.

My first assignment with the symphony was to review the governance process for the CSO, which led to an invitation to join the board. I served as vice-chair of the board responsible for oversight of finances for eight years. We eliminated the annual deficit of $1.5 million and operated with a small surplus. People are more willing to contribute to financially successful organizations than to fund deficits. We launched the renovation of our 100-year-old hall into a modern masterpiece with classic beauty and spectacular acoustics. We reorganized the board, instituted rotation at the top, and altered governance. The changes were important, as the CSO continues to grapple with changes in attitudes toward classical music among the younger generations.

As a trustee of Rush University Medical Center (RUMC), I was the first chair of the new Alzheimer's Center and subsequently chair of Rush University during my nearly forty years of board service with Rush. RUMC has become one of the top research and clinical medical centers in the country. It spends $250 million per year on free medical care for the poor, subsidies for Medicaid, and community service. Rush is a shining example of American healthcare at its best, ranking among the top few medical centers in the country on important quality measures. Its new hospital is a model for hospitals of the future and an example of why healthcare belongs in the private sector. Most recently, Rush is pioneering community wellness in Chicago and is the beta test for a new government-sponsored initiative to handle vets in private hospitals rather than the VA hospital system. I continue as a life trustee and member of two committees.

The Chicago Central Area Committee fostered changes in our downtown area to make it more vibrant and serviceable to those who lived, worked, and visited there. Bruce Graham, who preceded me as chair of the Central Area Committee, was one of the world's premier architects and head of Skidmore, Owings & Merrill. Graham developed a plan to convert downtown Chicago from a nine-to-five business center into a 24/7 mecca of entertainment, business, and commercial activity and one of the most attractive residential areas of the city. Wacker Drive, LaSalle Street, and North Michigan Avenue have been transformed into beautiful boulevards with flowers and trees down their centers. The River Walk bordering the Chicago River as it winds through downtown replaced grungy docks and warehouses. The River Walk might not rival the banks of the Seine in Paris, but it makes a beautiful statement for a Midwest city in America. Take a boat trip down the Chicago River and you will marvel at the extraordinary architecture, a harmonious blend of stately old buildings with remarkably creative architecture of the past forty years. Downtown, River North, and the near South Side have seen an extraordinary construction boom and have attracted more than 200,000 residents, mostly young professionals. Great restaurants, theater, and new hotels have followed.

The Chicago Council on Foreign Relations (now the Chicago Council on Global Affairs) was the first civic board I joined in Chicago because of my interest in international affairs. Ultimately, I served as chairman for three years and continue as a life trustee. We developed a new strategy for the council and revised its governance process and programming to attract more young professionals. One of the most memorable highlights of my board tenure was our lengthy meeting with President Nelson Mandela during a council board trip to South Africa.

While I was chair of the Visiting Committee on Public Policy Studies at the University of Chicago, we recommended that a School of Public Policy Studies be established—the first new school for the University of Chicago since the founding of the medical school in 1932. Thanks to Irving Harris, a fellow board member, the Harris School is vibrant and thriving.

Jim O'Conner was asked by Cardinal Joseph Bernardin to establish the Big Shoulders Fund to save the Catholic school system in the inner city from almost certain financial collapse. I have served on his board for thirty-five years. The fund has raised over $450 million and offers the best hope for a bright future to children from the poorest neighborhoods in Chicago. The results—measured by percentages of children who graduate from high school and four-year colleges—are extraordinary compared with other kids from the same neighborhoods and economic status in public schools. Visiting these inner-city schools in some of Chicago's toughest neighborhoods makes you believe that these children are not lost and have a real shot at productive, satisfying lives. Big Shoulders has been one of our most important charities since its inception.

Outside Chicago, I have served on several boards, including the board of The Thunderbird School of International Management, for ten years, five as chairman. The student body was one-third American, one-third Latin American, and one-third Asian and European—a virtual United Nations in Glendale, Arizona. In my final year, I gave the commencement address ("Dream Big") and received an honorary doctorate of International Law.

I have served on the board of the Brookings Institution—the number one–ranked think tank in the world—for over twenty-five years, eight on the executive committee. I have loved getting to know and working with the scholars, some of the brightest people anywhere. I joined the University of Notre Dame's Mendoza School of Business Advisory Board about twenty years ago to strengthen my relationship with my alma mater. Mendoza has a program, Business on the Front Lines (BoFL), in which students go to countries emerging from extreme conditions to help people, such as former drug gang members in Colombia, create small businesses. I have been helping them bring BoFL to Chicago. Other educational boards included Marymount of Paris and St. Ignatius College Preparatory School.

TechnoServe, where I served for five years, was founded in the late 1960s by an American businessman who believed that the poor villagers in Ghana where he was living as a missionary and healthcare worker were as inherently smart and potentially capable as he was, but they didn't have the necessary information to start or build businesses. TechnoServe is a not-for-profit consulting company devoted to helping local people in poor, developing countries establish and grow private small businesses—to enable poor people to transform their own lives through their own efforts. Today TechnoServe works in over forty countries across the globe and has a huge impact on individual lives and on developing economies by building their private sectors. I visited a few field projects, such as one in San Salvador, and saw firsthand how effectively they coached locals to get businesses up and running successfully. Few NGOs have development records that match TechnoServe's.

Serving on boards that help your community or society is immensely satisfying.

OUR FAMILY PARTNERSHIP

Mitzi and I approached community service as a partnership. We have both been committed to it, though she was much better than I during our early years and while living overseas. I was traveling nonstop. In Brazil, she taught full-time in a local Catholic elementary school as a volunteer and inaugurated and headed a language arts department. In France, Mitzi was awarded the Silver Medal of Paris for her work as president of the American Women's Group of Paris and building French-American relations. She was also awarded a Medal of Honor from Vieilles Maisons Françaises. In Chicago, she served on several boards but made her real mark with the Children's Home and Aid Society of Illinois (CHASI)—an organization serving over 40,0000 disadvantaged kids and families in tough neighborhoods throughout the state. Over a thirty-year period, she led the Women's Board, chaired CHASI's board, and was the catalyst for the creation of the Mitzi Freidheim Englewood Child and Family Center in one of Chicago's most dangerous neighborhoods. The center serves two hundred kids aged one to five with preschool activities and a crisis nursery, and provides education and counseling to 350 families. They received a national award for their "Power to Fathers" program. Currently, Mitzi serves as a trustee of the Lost Tree Foundation; she volunteers teaching reading to underprivileged children in the Riviera Beach community . . . and has become a Dame in the Order of Malta.

We are grateful that our children have also been active in community service on boards and have contributed their time and money to important causes. Lynn left her commercial career to work with UNICEF, as she wanted to do something more meaningful. When she moved to London to get married, she joined Sadler's Wells. Now with three children, she volunteers with their schools and is president of her brother's foundation. Stephen set up a foundation devoted to "Opening doors through education and knowledge" and asked his sister, brother, and parents to join him and his wife, Amandine, on the board. Stephen also sits on the boards of the Council of Foreign Relations, the Peterson Institute for International Economics, the U.S. Olympic and Paralympic Foundation, and Yale University. Scott has served on a number of national and local not-for-profit boards such as the Institute for International Education (manager of the Fulbright awards), Spellman College, and the U.S. Olympic and Paralympic Foundation . . . and is a Knight of the Order of Malta. Amandine has thrown herself into community service since she was eleven, raising money for a school in Senegal. She went on a college internship working for a hospital in Vietnam and an exchange program in Cuernavaca, Mexico, raising funds for poor kids. Now with three children, she volunteers for several organizations in New York and serves on the board of Partnership Schools. Amandine is a Dame of Malta.

We all continue to devote our time to working for causes we believe in deeply. Many of the friends Mitzi and I have made over the years stemmed from our involvement in community organizations. I learned a lot about people, about how organizations work, about leadership, about the needs of society, and about how to solve problems that seem intransigent. Our children say the same about their involvements.

SIX RULES

Let me share six rules developed from my years working as a member of civic, educational, and charitable organizations:

1. **Join only those organizations whose mission, values, ethics, effectiveness, and reputation are consistent with your interests and values. Do careful due diligence before joining.** If you are not interested in their activities, don't join. Don't go near organizations that don't meet your ethical standards.

2. **Select organizations that are a good match for your knowledge and skills.** Look closely at the board to assure yourself you are a good fit for each other both professionally and personally. Have positive reasons for joining.

3. **Understand the organization's expectations of a board member and what you are asked to bring to the table.** Many organizations primarily want your money, and in some cases it's too much. Or the group may want too much of your time. Avoid future embarrassment; ask up-front what is expected. And if you're not sure, work on a project or a committee before you commit to board service.

4. **Be willing and able to become involved in important ways.** Commit the time and energy necessary to deliver value to the organization. Have impact. Exceed their expectations. Exceed your own. Don't join unless you can and will.

5. **If the circumstances change either for you or the organization that alter your view of the organization negatively or your willingness and ability to be associated with it, resign gracefully.** Don't linger because of inertia.

6. **If there is an important need in your community that isn't being met by existing organizations, consider creating an organization to fill the gap.** The success of your involvement with one or two organizations will lead to invitations to join other groups.

The true spirit of any city, and certainly a driver of Chicago's greatness, is involvement of its citizens and leaders in the community. The business community populates the civic, educational, and charity boards in Chicago. When the Civic Committee or Commercial Club meets, almost every major not-for-profit organization in the city is represented. That's because the business community truly is dedicated to making Chicago a great place to do business, raise a family, and live happily. The Civic Committee is a cohesive group of friends who like and respect each other. New members are welcomed and don't have to fight their way into the inner circle, as is the case in most cities.

In my view, Chicago has a model worthy of imitation.

Mitzi and I have invested heavily in Chicago with our time, our talent, and financially over the past forty years. I know we made a difference; we wish we could have done more. We have never regretted spending our time "giving back," because of the enormous satisfaction of having a positive impact on a city we loved and called home.

My advice: Start small but get involved. Commit and Deliver.

Chapter Ten

RETIREMENT

"Better to Wear Out Than Rust Out"

Retirement is a stage in life we both fear and look forward to. The fear comes from the unknowns: What will I do? Will I have enough money? How will my health be? There are hundreds of books on retirement: how to plan for it; how to save and invest for it. Read them if you must. I am sure there is good advice. My intent here is simply to describe how I approached retirement and what happened. The lessons at the end are in retrospect with 20/20 hindsight. I didn't foresee what would happen, but those lessons capture what I learned.

LOST TREE VILLAGE

We began thinking about retirement when we returned from Europe in 1979. I was in my forties and a long way from retirement. We decided to look for a small apartment in southeast Florida as an escape from northern winters. We chose Florida because we both loved the climate and thought Florida might be the place we would retire. So this would be a trial run.

As a compulsive consultant, I studied the area exhaustively. We decided on a small gated community, Lost Tree Village, in North Palm Beach on the Atlantic Ocean about eight miles north of Palm Beach. Lost Tree was populated with 500-plus business and professional leaders, about half of whom were retired. It had a nice golf course, a number of tennis courts, and a very active social and cultural life. We had stumbled into one of the best—from our perspective—communities in Florida.

Lost Tree quickly became vacation central for the family and has remained so for thirty-five years as the family welcomed three wonderful spouses and nine grandchildren into the fold. We moved from our original modest house on the golf course to Mitzi's dream house on Lake Worth as we neared retirement. We became Florida residents and spend eight months a year in Lost Tree. Our first step toward retirement—finding a great place to live—was accomplished.

It's never too early to think about where you will retire. Pick a place you love to be and your family will love to visit.

Sister Jean (Dolores Schmidt), a 100-year-old nun, became a national celebrity a few years ago when she was adopted by Loyola University's basketball team as their chaplain. Loyola made the NCAA tournament for the first time in memory and went to the Final Four on the spirit of Sister Jean. I met her a year later and commented on her extraordinary energy—she attended almost all their games. Her response: "Better to wear out than rust out."

As I approached retirement from Booz Allen after thirty-five-plus years, I had time to think about a number of things that I wanted to do professionally, personally, and in the community. My intent was to take my time deciding with which organizations to engage and how to allocate my time. The first two years were an unexpected detour, totally absorbed by Chiquita. Clearly an exciting chapter in my life.

Stay active.

RETIREMENT II

As the end of my two-year commitment with Chiquita approached, we initiated the search for a new CEO, and planning began for Retirement II. I was approaching my sixty-ninth birthday, so my bucket list was a bit less ambitious. The biggest items were to get grandchildren (which was unfortunately outside my control), to contribute more time to organizations important to us, to travel, to write another book, and to restore my golf game. Again, I was sidetracked—this time into the political world to help re-elect President George W. Bush. Mitzi and I became Regents with the Republican National Committee (RNC). I was adopted by Al Hoffman, who was chair of finance for the RNC. Al involved me in the campaign and with fundraising.

I loved the meetings with the president and senior government officials and discussions about policy . . . and truly disliked fundraising. Hoffman became a good friend, and even today we work together to support candidates and causes we believe in. I strongly believe that involvement by citizens in the electoral process is important in a democracy and that your voice does matter if you participate. We have been active in every national election since 2004. Our candidates for Congress and the presidency have not always won; but with one exception, all have deserved our support.

The 2008 election occurred while I was the publisher of the *Chicago Sun-Times*, which gave me a platform for discussing issues and meeting with candidates, including a long interview with Senator Barack Obama, but prohibited fundraising or financially supporting any candidates or party.

Sister Jean said, "I don't believe you get things done by yelling, screaming, and holding up signs." Get involved in the political process as early as you can. Make your voice matter.

After the 2004 election, I had discussions and interviews for potential roles with the government, but nothing materialized. Finally, I got serious about deciding what to do with the rest of my life. As I exited

Chiquita, I continued to serve on the HSBC USA board and was invited to join the board of Allegheny Energy. I also continued working with Brookings Institution, Chicago Symphony Orchestra, Rush University Medical Center, the Chicago Council on Global Affairs, and Big Shoulders, and joined the boards of the Lost Tree Property Owners' Association and Mendoza School of Business at the University of Notre Dame.

My first task was to pay more attention to these organizations. For example, I became lead director for both HSBC USA and Allegheny Energy and took on active committee assignments with the other organizations. I was interested in adding one or two commercial boards, but my age was against me. The biggest change was to join Mitzi more frequently in Florida for the winter. We had made a commitment to spend seven months a year at Lost Tree when I retired from Booz Allen. Mitzi lived up to her commitment; but Chiquita and Cincinnati intervened, so I didn't keep my commitment. Now it was time for me to step up. And maybe get my old golf game back? I was ready.

Two years later, another unexpected detour appeared in my plan. I joined the board of Hollinger International and a year later became the CEO of the Sun-Times Media Group. That same summer, Stephen invited me to join the board of Virgin America, an investment that Cyrus Capital was making to fund a start-up airline in the United States. Suddenly, I had two additional commercial boards. Golf was proving to be an enjoyable but hopeless pursuit, and I welcomed another set of professional challenges.

Keep an open mind to unexpected opportunities. This lesson applies throughout your life.

Even though I was a few months short of seventy-four years old when I left the Sun-Times Media Group, real retirement seemed unlikely. My psyche couldn't handle a life of leisure, nor would Mitzi enjoy an idle husband under her feet. My health and mental state were still strong, so climbing another small mountain was not out of the question. There are countless people who continue to contribute to society well into their seventies and eighties. I view those decades as a gift to do something extra with life. All who are blessed with a healthy life beyond their last jobs have that opportunity. Being a septuagenarian does not mean useless or hopeless or inactive. My top priority was "Family First." Lynn, Stephen, and Scott were just married, and grandchildren were coming. That meant time with our kids and grandkids, both at Lost Tree and away, and more time with Mitzi doing what she wanted.

My second priority was to continue to be an effective contributor to the boards and organizations on which I was serving. HSBC USA had wound down, and I departed the Sun-Times Media board. That left Allegheny Energy and Virgin America and limited involvement with other organizations, but no prospects for major commitments elsewhere.

Again out of the blue, I was asked to join the board of the Lost Tree Club. One of my personal rules while actively working was to avoid club boards. They take up wicked amounts of time and can get involved in touchy personal matters. In this case, declining was difficult. We had enjoyed our wonderful village and club for thirty years. The quality of life there depended on its members contributing their time and talent. Time to do my part. I accepted, went to work developing a strategy for the club, and three years later was elected president of the club. And as I expected, it took a wicked amount of time and did get into touchy personal matters. The experience overall, however, was very satisfying. We implemented the strategy and put in place several programs to make our club a true family club.

Lost Tree is a special place where energetic and accomplished people enjoy a beautiful life together in a culture of deep respect and generosity for their community, the staff, and one another.

Helping your community takes many forms. It is so much better than complaining from the sidelines.

As I approached eighty, my children asked me to write a memoir of my life for my grandchildren. They argued that my young grandchildren would never get to know me. Luke, my first grandchild, came along when I was seventy-three. *Notes from Grampa* was one of the most satisfying projects of my very active retirement. It took almost three years. I recommend it for every grandfather and wish my grandfathers had written their stories.

Commit & Deliver is an offshoot of *Notes from Grampa*. I enjoy writing and have several ideas for additional books. *The Star of Africa*, my next book, is being considered by publishers now. There is no reason to stop, and I would certainly rather "wear out than rust out."

My retirement years have been full and exciting. I didn't recount the trips to Europe each summer, the countless wonderful hours with our nine grandchildren, the hyper-active social life Mitzi organizes in Florida and everywhere we go, the new and old friendships that enrich our lives and keep us intellectually engaged, relearning bridge, reading, exercising, playing occasional golf, and allowing naps from time to time. Most of what I have done was not even thought about when I was planning retirement. I have been fortunate to have reasonably good health (despite four joint replacements and a redo of my spine) and a loving wife and family. I will always remember my dad's final advice: "Family is the most important thing in life. In the end, family is all that really matters."

In retrospect, my counsel is to plan ahead but let life take you in directions you hadn't planned. Here are six guidelines for planning your retirement with the benefit of 20/20 hindsight:

- Stay Active . . . Better to wear out than rust out.
- Build a financial nest that allows you to do what you want—not lavishly but without worrying about the rent. Don't count on Social Security. It may not be there for you.
- Decide where to live. Pick a place you will love to be and your family will want to visit, a place that will enhance your life.
- Think about what types of things you really enjoy doing. Write them down, but in pencil with an eraser. Be open to the unexpected: Do it if you believe it will excite you but don't be afraid to say "no."
- Keep physically and mentally healthy, not in a nutty way, but recognize that age takes its toll on everyone.
- Faith, family, and friends are your best allies.

YOU ARE YOUR MOST IMPORTANT PROJECT

My preparation for life began at home as soon as I could talk and observe, and culminated with my graduation from business school. My military service enabled me to begin life without guardrails and support from my parents and schools and to give myself a liberal education during those four years. My business career played out over the following fifty. An active retirement followed. My education has never stopped.

Probably the most important lesson to pass to following generations is from General James "Mad Dog" Mattis, who headed the Marine Corps and served as Secretary of Defense: *"Take responsibility for your life and your career."* You are unique and only you can determine who and what you will become.

Throughout this book, I have drawn lessons from my experiences. Many have been learned the hard way—through mistakes. But every experience, good or bad, counts and should make us wiser. I hope you can gain from those lessons without having to make the same mistakes. Seven pieces of advice summarize what I wished was engraved on my psyche throughout my career. If they are helpful, I will have achieved the most important goal of writing this book.

1. **Keep a strong moral compass**

   Early in life, make up your mind what kind of person you want to become—not what career you will follow, but rather the character and reputation you wish to have. Then dedicate yourself to being that person. Given that challenge, most people will choose a path of integrity, honesty, generosity, fairness, kindness, and other virtues. The tough part is living up to those ideals. The secret is to begin with the little things by asking, "What is the right thing to do?" You will be tested early. An example is cheating—on a test in school or taking more than your fair share or marking a five on a hole in golf knowing that you really had a six. Another example is lying—to avoid punishment, to make yourself look better, to give yourself an advantage.

   If you discipline yourself to be strong on the little things, you will be able to be strong when the really important challenges face you later in life. You will make mistakes and disappoint yourself and others close to you. When that happens, understand what you did wrong and correct it.

   People will know you through your words and actions. Make sure your words and actions communicate the person you want to be. Developing a strong moral compass takes work and discipline. Never sell yourself or your principles for any price. Do not permit yourself to be coerced into doing something you think is wrong or not right for you. Do not do something just to please others or avoid criticism. Most likely it will turn out badly for you. Make your own decisions. Take responsibility for your life. Courage requires emotional not physical strength.

2. Serve

In chapter nine on boards, the case is made that everyone has an obligation to help the disadvantaged and that obligation grows significantly with your financial success and talent. If you aren't yet convinced, please reread that chapter, go someplace private and silent, and think about it.

There is an important application of the service mentality in your careers. In my experience, the best and most effective leaders in any field are those who view their role as serving their organizations, their employees, their customers/clients, and their society. Jim Allen wrote a brief booklet, *The Spirit of Service*, which was distributed to every new consultant at Booz Allen. The booklet defined what service to clients and the community meant and how we could embrace it. *The Spirit of Service* defined the culture of the firm. "Understand what is important to them (clients, friends, associates, community leaders) and help them achieve it."

Service-driven leaders work *for* their employees and customers. They understand that using the talents and creativity in the whole organization is far more effective than relying on a few top people. The service-driven leader has confidence in people and values their judgment and work. A few simple rules/guidelines:

- The leader's most important job is to tap the potential of every member of the organization by providing support and removing obstacles to doing their jobs effectively.
- The leader takes responsibility, but not the credit.
- Recognition of achievement is a powerful motivator.

This mindset applies to every job you will have—from project leader with two team members to CEO of a large organization. David Novak, former CEO of Yum! Brands, has written several books on the power of recognition.

3. **Do what you love, love what you do**

No one achieves greatness at something they don't feel passionate about. Being great at anything requires focus, commitment, discipline, energy, and dedication. You don't get bored or tired doing what you love. You don't count or begrudge the hours of effort. You take risks to make things better and are quick to recover when you misstep. You will receive life's greatest rewards: satisfaction, self-respect, and the respect of others who matter most to you.

Corollary: Love it or leave it.

You are the artist and architect of your life. Every artist starts with a blank canvas. Imagination, creativity, talent, and determination separate the giants from the amateurs.

Sister Jean stated it more directly: "If you don't like your work, you're a pain to yourself and everyone else, so get another job."

4. **Never quit**

Never give up. You will fall, you will fail, you will be disappointed, you will disappoint. Always pick yourself up, get back on your horse, and ride on with your head held high. Figure out why you fell short and resolve to do better. I know of no successful person who has never failed or met a seemingly impossible challenge in their lives and careers.

The people I admire the most are those who have fallen hardest or faced the worst challenges and found a way to come back from the ashes and win big. These include a young man who was thrown out of college as a freshman but clawed his way back to graduate and have the medical career he had dreamed about. These include the war veteran who lost both legs in Afghanistan but refused to consider himself a victim and is now a member of Congress. These include a young woman who lost her legs in a train accident as a teenager but refused to end her dream of becoming a world-famous concert violinist. These include a poor black child whose illiterate single mother forced him to learn (and eventually love) to read and refused to think of her family as victims. She saw her son become the most famous pediatric surgeon in the world and run for president. These include the countless entrepreneurs who failed time and again before getting it right. These include the alcoholics, addicts, sinners, and criminals who recognize they have lost their way and reform. These are my heroes.

The common denominator—they never quit. If you give up it's over. That applies to your personal life as well as your career.

5. **Treat everyone with respect, but choose your friends and associates carefully**

Every human being deserves to be treated with respect. The Declaration of Independence and every religion have it right: *All people are created equal and have the unalienable right to life, liberty, and the pursuit of happiness.* We are all God's children. Treat everyone with respect—regardless of who they are, what they look like, where they come from, what they believe, what their political or social views are, rich or poor, strong or weak, young or old, smart or dumb, saints or felons, friends or enemies . . . regardless even of what they did to you or said about you. Treat them *all* with respect. The cost is low, but the benefits are enormous. Dale Carnegie wrote a bestseller in 1936, *How to Win Friends and Influence People,* based on that one principle: Treat everyone with respect. What a better place the world would be if everyone followed Carnegie's advice. If you are interested, Carnegie's book is compelling and a quick read.

On the other hand, not all people merit your trust. Pick your friends and associates with care. The closer they are to you, the more care you should exercise.

Marry the right person . . . or don't get married. That person will be responsible for 90 percent of the joy or misery in your life. That person should share the same values and principles that guide your life. Pick someone who makes you laugh and laughs with you . . . who takes care of you and lets you take care of them . . . who wants what is best for you . . . who is positive and focuses on what is possible . . . who wants to be happy . . . who wants to raise a family with you. Finally, do not mistake infatuation for love . . . or physical beauty for inner beauty.

Throughout your life, build a cadre of friends and associates who share your values, who have earned your respect, whose company you enjoy, who make you better when you are with them. Keep contact with them even if your lives go in separate ways. You can never have too many friends and associates who meet those criteria. Times will come when those friends and associates can play important roles in your life. A Rolodex of outstanding people can be invaluable when starting a new venture or helping you back on your feet or populating your White House staff.

Seek mentors throughout your life. Pick people whose values and character you respect. Pick people who are interested in you, who will put your best interests ahead of their own, who have experiences or skills from which you can benefit, with whom you can build a bond of trust. Start with your parents and family, such as uncles and aunts or a grampa or grammy; get close to a teacher or coach; pick a boss or colleague at work who meets these standards. You will benefit from good mentors at every stage in your life. Also be generous with your time and pick young people to mentor yourself.

Be fair and respectful but tough with your critics. Every one of us has met somebody who doesn't like us. And sometimes that person may be in a position to do us harm. Do not let that deter you. Do what you must to prevail but maintain your principles. Don't be afraid to stand up for yourself, but don't make unnecessary enemies.

Be kind. Be nice, as my granddaughter Juliette puts it. Kindness and civility are vastly underrated qualities in modern society. Forgive often and generously. Give credit when earned. Recognition is one of a leader's most valuable tools. Let others give you credit rather than claiming credit for yourself. It takes courage to be kind; courage comes from the mind and heart, not from physical strength.

6. **Believe**

Belief is a gift. The difference between humans and all other creatures on Earth is the ability to think rationally and to believe. How you embrace this gift will have an enormous impact on your life now and probably beyond. Belief is based on knowledge without proof. We believe in people we love. We believe in God. Most religions teach us to believe in a life after death.

My counsel to you is to *believe in something beyond yourself,* beyond the here and now. A strong spiritual life will put more meaning into everything you do. It will strengthen your commitment to build your character, to avoid temptations to go off track, to remain faithful to your principles, to help others who are not as blessed, to be humble about your achievements, to pick yourself up after you have failed. I was lucky to be raised in a family of committed Catholics in which faith was a given. My faith was strengthened in Catholic grammar school, high school, and college. I know the value of religion and am deeply grateful for the gift of belief.

Believe in yourself. Believe you can accomplish a task and your odds of doing it rise immeasurably. Believe you can get good grades, make the team, get the job you dreamed about, earn a promotion, start a business, have a great family, be a good person . . . and you will. Self-confidence is good, even infectious. Just watch out that it doesn't become arrogance and isn't based on an inaccurate self-assessment. Self-confidence allows you to be yourself without constantly trying to prove how good or smart you are, without boasting or bragging.

Believe in your principles. If you have done your job of defining the person you want to become and laid out the principles that will get you there, it will be easy to have faith in those principles—particularly when they are challenged or you are tempted.

Believe in your family. You will be tested when a member of your family strays off track or hurts you. Give them the benefit of the doubt and do everything you can to bring them back into the fold. Remember Family First, which means in good times and bad.

7. **Commit and Deliver**

The title and theme of this book is *Commit & Deliver*. It is a philosophy of life. It is a roadmap for a successful career. It is a standard of behavior. It builds character. It builds relationships, it earns respect, it applies to your personal life and every job you will ever have, it applies to every rung of the ladder you wish to climb. My suggestion: Adopt this philosophy and live it. Life will be better.

Those are my seven pieces of advice for you to consider. They won't guarantee financial success—although they will help. They won't cover all circumstances and challenges you face. They will help you achieve a happy, useful life, and help you become the person you want to be.

Throughout our lives, we are all confronted with difficult decisions, difficult choices. The toughest are those where the stakes are high, the right answer is unclear or doesn't exist, and thoughtful people argue both sides. In all difficult choices the correct course is to understand the facts, arguments, and options (there may be few or there may be dozens) and act on your conclusion of what is right. If it is your decision to make, you must make it, even if others whom you respect, trust, or even love disagree with you. It is your decision. You have to live with it and face the final judge. If you have done what you truly believe was right, you will be fine.

I have had my chance to make the world a better place in my eighty-plus years. Now it is your turn to lead in the future. If not you, then who?

Good luck.

ACKNOWLEDGMENTS

My first acknowledgment is to my two families—the one I was born into and the one Mitzi and I created. Each family member has had a major influence on me and helped me become who I am. I do, however, take full credit for my mistakes. I have been fortunate to have two supportive, loving families.

Next are the schools and the Catholic Church, which taught me the values, discipline, and foundation of learning that lasted a lifetime: St. Philip Neri in South Shore, Chicago; St. Ignatius College Preparatory School in one of the toughest areas of Chicago at that time; the University of Notre Dame in South Bend, Indiana; and Carnegie Institute of Technology (now Carnegie Mellon University) in Pittsburgh, Pennsylvania. So many nuns, priests, teachers, professors, and coaches supported me and showed me the right direction. So many gave me the benefit of the doubt and the confidence to achieve what I thought was unattainable.

The U.S. Navy and the many organizations with which I have worked as an employee, a director, a consultant, and a volunteer all taught me valuable lessons that allowed me to continue to grow throughout my long career. Countless colleagues and bosses took the time to guide me, even when I didn't think I needed it, and to pick me up when I stumbled. Of particular significance were my years with Booz Allen Hamilton, whose values and standards of integrity, fairness, objectivity, and discipline forged my character. A special acknowledgment goes to my assistant of twenty-two years at Booz Allen, Vicki Anderson, who saved me countless times and made me look better than I deserved. An assistant like Vicki can be the best ally in your career.

Special recognition to my mentors throughout my life—my parents, who knew just when and how to notch up the pressure; Rev. Ed Barron at St. Philip Neri, who understood that all kids made mistakes and that setting high expectations was far more effective than punishment in getting them on the right path; Revs. Esmaker and Shanley at St. Ignatius, who knew how to control and motivate teenagers; Fr. Dan O'Neill, a port in many storms at Notre Dame; Harold Leavitt and Leland Hazzard at Carnegie Mellon, who coached their intern to think like an executive. In my business career, my most important mentors were Bill Sick and Allan Gilmore at Ford; Jim Allen, Jim Farley, and John Rhodes at Booz Allen; and Don Perkins, Don Clark, and John Richman in community activities and boards.

Many others have taught me how important each of us can be in making our society and communities better through their extraordinary contributions, particularly Jim O'Connor, Msgr. Ken Velo, and Lester Crown. Every client and every CEO with whom I worked taught me important lessons. The full list of mentors is probably tenfold those mentioned. I was fortunate to learn early on that listening to wise and trusted friends and mentors was one of the best sources of advice widely available but too rarely tapped.

Responsibility for persuading me to write *Commit & Deliver* and *Notes from Grampa* belongs to Mitzi, Lynn, Stephen, and Scott, who were relentless in telling me that I had to leave the lessons of my life and career to my grandchildren. Stephen brought in Bob Dilenschneider and his editorial team to guide me professionally and help this novice produce a book. My family, along with Bob Dilenschneider, Phil Revzin, and Chris Fortunato, were my editorial board, fact checkers, and provocateurs, keeping me in bounds on *Commit & Deliver*. Special thanks to Bob for his continuous encouragement and to Phil for drawing heavily from his decades-long editorial experience with *The Wall Street Journal* to make my stories shorter and more to the point. Sophia Franco provided a mountain of support with her research.

Finally, and most important, was the inspiration and support for the past sixty years of my life partner, Mitzi. Mitzi raised three almost perfect children, encouraged and supported me in good and not so good times, and pulled up stakes and moved countless times, instilling excitement in all of us for each new adventure. Mitzi has made my life far more enjoyable, productive, and successful than I imagined or deserved. At the same time, Mitzi devoted herself to causes she believed in, becoming a leader in virtually everything she undertook, and living the values and principles of her faith as a beautiful model for her family and all who have known her.

INDEX

ABOUT THE AUTHOR

Cyrus Freidheim wrote *Notes from Grampa* for his grandchildren. He wrote *Commit & Deliver* for others who wish to pursue a career in business or are midstream in their careers and wondering, "Is that is all there is?" In both books, he wants to "pour into your minds as much of what I have learned as possible." Raised in an Irish-Catholic neighborhood on the South Side of Chicago, he graduated from the University of Notre Dame and served four years in the U.S. Navy, where he became an interpreter in Russian. He earned an MBA at Carnegie Mellon University. He claims the best decision in his life was marrying Mitzi, and together they raised three almost perfect children.

Freidheim's business career began at Union Carbide and Price Waterhouse, followed by Ford Motor, Booz Allen Hamilton, Chiquita Brands International, and Sun-Times Media Group. He served on fifteen corporate boards and twenty-plus not-for-profit boards—five as chairman. He worked in over twenty-five countries and on every continent except Antarctica, assisting and running companies undergoing major transformations or turnarounds.

Freidheim and his wife now live in Lost Tree Village, a small community in southeast Florida populated with an active group of current and former business, professional, and government leaders. Their nine grandchildren all hold two passports, travel frequently between the United States and Europe, and are becoming world citizens of the next generation.